Heiser's Essential Guide to

Shooting Vintage Rifles in Australia

Paul Heiser

Copyright © 2024 Paul Heiser

Paul Heiser's right to be identified as the author of this work has been asserted by him under the Copyright Amendment (Moral Rights) Act 2000

All rights reserved. No portion of this publication maybe reproduced, stored in a retrieval system, or transmitted in any form or by any means: electronic, mechanical, photocopied, recorded or otherwise, without express written permission from the author and the publisher.

ISBN 978-0-6456819-4-9 (paperback)

Printed in Australia

First edition February 2025

Disclaimer

The author and publisher have no control over the reader's firearms, the reader's knowledge about the reloading of firearms, how the reader will use this information, or the materials and components the reader will use. All information in this book should be approached with, and used with, caution. The author and publisher assume no responsibility for the use of this information.

Contents

Dedication	VII
Preface	1
Acknowledgements	3
1. Shooting vintage firearms	5
2. Shooting Muzzleloading Firearms	11
3. Skills and techniques of loading cartridges	24
4. Loading the Cartridge	37
5. Choosing a Mould	44
6. Cast Projectiles	54
7. Black Powder Cartridges	71
8. Obsolete and Vintage Smokeless Cartridges	80
9. Cleaning Firearms and Cases	84
10. Final Words	97

Appendices	101
Bibliography	125

*To my late mother Marguerite Heiser
who said I should write a book,
and to my wife Anne
who inspired me to do so.*

Preface

I started writing this book, firstly to collate my articles and organise the information in some semblance of order, and secondly, for my own amusement with no determined will to see it published. It was an act of self-discipline; an attempt to prove that I would not give up halfway, and have another incomplete project on my conscience.

My interest in firearms developed from playing with my plastic toy soldiers – a gift from my maternal grandmother – as a pre-schooler. Later on, schooling fostered my love of the written word and history. I was blessed with a good memory for anything I was interested in, and a total lack of recall for the foundations of algebra and quadratic equations. I wanted to know when a Brown Bess was used, and the difference between Snider Enfields, Martini Enfields and Lee Enfields. Vintage firearms called out to me like sirens on the rocks, and I was lured.

An author whom I admire once said that regardless of the length of his books, he restricts his preface to just two pages. He contended that if you could not introduce what was written in two pages, you probably did not fully understand your own subject matter. Who am I to go against the words of a more learned and published author?

Far too many vintage firearms languish unused because their ammunition is not easily available or long discontinued; you may not be able to obtain suitable projectiles for it, or reloading dies cannot be sourced. Unfortunately, many present-day shooters do not persevere to understand the fundamentals of what is required to get these old girls up and running.

My hope is that this book will encourage you to go beyond your comfort zone and experience the fun, folly and occasional frustration at reloading and discharging a Snider, Martini or Gras - rather than relegating it to a curio which spends its life in a safe.

Paul Heiser
Norman Park, Queensland, Australia

Acknowledgements

I would like to thank Michael Greenhill and Robert Finlay who proofread the early text for any glaring errors and anomalies.

There is much information available to the shooter, some of it is erroneous, some dangerous, and some are pearls to be kept, cherished and continually referred to. The advent of the internet greatly enhanced the information available to shooters. To all those who freely gave their time and knowledge, thank you.

To the many shooting companions who mentored me and showed me the correct method of shooting, reloading and preserving firearms – thank you.

I would also like to thank the Sporting Shooters Association of Australia (Qld.) Inc. who, in 2000 after requests from collectors, took what was probably a gamble and formed the Historical Arms Collectors Branch. It was the continual need for material for the branch newsletter which set me on my journey of writing articles.

Chapter One

Shooting vintage firearms

Whether you use black powder cartridge, obsolete centrefire cartridge firearms or muzzleloaders, there are common threads for shooting these firearms, particularly with regard to safety. Moreover, each type of firearm has its own peculiar requirements for loading and maintenance that will be examined in later chapters.

Let us start with muzzleloaders that fall into three subtypes: matchlocks, flintlocks and percussion. Matchlocks are amongst the most primitive forms of firearm, utilising a simple pivoted trigger with an attached slow burning fuse; pulling the trigger places the fuse against a touch hole on the barrel that is primed with black powder. Early matchlocks used the firer's hand to bring the burning end of the fuse to the flash hole, and did not even have a trigger. By the time of the English Civil War (1642-1651) the elementary trigger system was standard. Though rudimentary - being little more than a pipe sealed at one end and attached to a stick - they performed well, and sounded the death knell of the pike, which now went the way of the longbow and crossbow. They changed the way the ordinary soldier fought on the battlefield, though their time of supremacy had already passed by the beginning of the eighteenth century. Any town dweller or agricultural labourer could be trained to operate a matchlock, as opposed to longbows which took many years of practise to reach proficiency. Matchlocks are not commercially manufactured for the modern shooter, but they do occasionally appear courtesy of a small band of enthusiasts who manufacture them. Original matchlocks are far too expensive to contemplate firing, and they would be over three hundred years old. One would need great faith in the quality of the metal in the barrel before attempting to fire an original matchlock.

Flintlocks replaced the matchlock and reigned supreme in the western hemisphere from around 1700 to 1840. The manufacture of flintlocks started as a cottage industry, and with the growth of the industrial revolution were eventually produced in what would be to us recognisable factories. The flintlock is inherently safer than the matchlock, as any burning material (such as a slow burning fuse) near black powder is cause for concern and caution. A piece of flint held between the jaws of the hammer was a more reliable method of ignition than a smouldering cord subject to weather conditions. Think of the poor hunter taking aim at a deer to feed his family, and just as he takes aim… rain douses the cord. And that is a benign example. Facing a charging carnivore intent on doing mischief to you risks far direr consequences.

Flintlocks can have either a smoothbore or rifled barrel, depending on the era they represent. Rifling was probably invented by German gunsmiths in the middle of the eighteenth century, and while rifled barrels were quickly acknowledged as superior to smoothbores, the rifled flintlock never replaced smoothbores. Napoleon had little time for rifles as he considered them too slow to load, and while the British did have elite rifle regiments that used rifles, they considered a smoothbore Brown Bess sporting a bayonet the best remedy for the King or Queen's enemy of the day. Perhaps they subconsciously pined for the pike used six generations earlier.

The shooter today has a large variety of replica flintlocks to choose from, ranging from quality North American and

European makers down to pieces of dubious virtue and safety made in third world countries.

We now come to the next stage of development of the muzzleloader: the replacement of the flint with a percussion cap. The percussion cap was invented by the Reverend Alexander Forsyth, a Scottish cleric who nearly blew himself into the afterlife whilst trying to develop a reliable cap that would replace the flint. Though too late for the Napoleonic wars, the percussion cap quickly made inroads on commercial firearms, and many flintlocks were converted to use them. Percussion caps were more reliable than the flint and, being used only once, must be considered an early example of an item manufactured to be disposable. Our throwaway society is nothing new.

I have to admit that the percussion capped military rifle is my favourite muzzleloader, and perhaps I am being biased when I say that the Parker Hale replica Enfield muskets made from 1972 until the early 1990s were the best quality off-the-shelf muzzleloaders ever made. However, to be objective, Pedersoli, Euroarms and Lyman make great muzzleloaders and you would not be disappointed with them. The enthusiast can choose between replica British, North American and continental martial firearms and replicas of fine fowling and hunting pieces. An interesting collection can be gathered that includes smoothbore flintlocks and finishes up with rifled percussion arms that represented the zenith of muzzleloading. Though not a fixed rule, price is often an indicator of quality, even when it comes to second-hand firearms. Always check, because what shines on the exterior may have a badly pitted barrel, or rust hidden on the interior of the lock. Occasionally, an original percussion cap muzzleloader in good condition does appear on the market. Its custodian must make an informed decision about whether to fire it or not.

Black powder cartridge firearms are the next step in firearm development, and offer more choice than muzzleloaders do. The market is driven by an insatiable demand in the United States for all things associated with the Wild West. It abounds with replica firearms from the Wild West, including Trapdoor Springfields, Sharps, Spencers, Rollingblocks, Henrys and Winchesters. The most popular calibre is 45.70, with too many books to mention written about this calibre. Two authors of particular note are Paul Matthews and Mike Venturino, and I recommend their books; however be prepared for some conflicting views on certain issues. If you prefer not to fire such a large calibre, well then try a 38.55 or a 44.40. Conversely, you may want to go in the other direction; if you yearn for a buffalo gun in 45.120, your dealer can get one in stock for you. For those of you who wish to shoot black powder cartridge rifles with a minimum of fuss and outlay, then go west young man (or woman)! You are spoilt for choice.

With black powder cartridge firearms other than those used in the Wild West, the choices are more limited. If you have a hankering to shoot Martini Henrys, Sniders or Model 71 Mausers, it is then a matter of finding an original in good condition, and doing some research on the internet and in books as to how other shooters tackled the task. Unfortunately, no one manufactures replicas of these firearms, so you will have to be organised and prepared to do hand loading and casting of projectiles (there is more on this in later chapters). As with muzzleloaders or any other firearm, you get what you pay for and bargains are few and far between. When shooting originals from the nineteenth century, keep in mind that broken extractors and firing pins may not be easily replaced or fabricated.

Chapter Two

Shooting Muzzleloading Firearms

The thing to keep in mind about shooting black powder, and particularly in regard to muzzleloaders, is that you will acquire accessories. Lots of accessories. Often in brass that will tarnish over time. You will also need various bits and bobs that will fit on the end of your cleaning rod or ramrod.

Because static electricity can cause black powder to ignite, equipment used in conjunction with black powder must not generate static electricity. The most popular material which meets this requirement is brass, followed by aluminium. Powder flasks, powder measures and cleaning rod attachments are generally made out of one of these two metals, with brass being the more common. Plastic generally creates static electricity, so plastics are rarely used although some brands of black powder are sold in antistatic plastic containers.

I can guarantee with absolute certainty that one day you will forget to load black powder into the barrel before loading your projectile. You will then need a certain attachment which is essentially a screw that fits on the end of your ramrod or cleaning rod, and you will wind the screw into the projectile until a firm grip is achieved, before pulling out the projectile. Likewise, when cleaning the barrel, the flannelette wrapped around your cleaning jag may come loose, especially if the flannelette is not moistened. In this instance an attachment resembling a one- or two-pronged corkscrew is essential for pulling out the offending piece of material. I prefer to have a ramrod for loading the projectile and a separate rod with a cleaning jag for running moistened flannelette up and down the barrel. Like the Boy Scout, be prepared and carry these essential pieces of equipment in your accessory bag when you are on the range... because one day, you **will** need them. Nothing is worse than having to cease shooting and go home early because you cannot remove an obstruction in your barrel.

One tip for the novice is to acquire ramrod accessories that are of a uniform fitting.

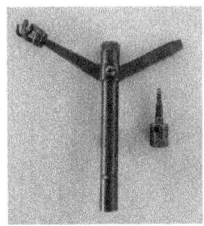

A Serjeant's Tool was issued to provide a practical tool that contained picks, pullet puller and worm and spring vice to effect minor repairs or remove stuck projectiles and wads.

Accessories are offered by different manufacturers in several different thread sizes and pitches, such as imperial 8-32, 10-32, 5/16 fittings and various metric threads. Just to complicate matters, these fittings are also offered in male and female fittings and unless you are careful, you will end up with accessories that require two or three different rods, and it is frustrating to have to take them all to the range. Where possible, take the time to acquire accessories that are all the same size in either a male or female fitting. 58 calibre and above fittings tend to be in the larger 10-32 or 5/16 threads, though conversion fittings are available so that, for instance, a 10-32 jag can be placed on a 8-32 rod.

Assuming that you have all the requisite pieces of equipment, let us start with firing a flintlock muzzleloader. I will restrict myself to firing modern day replicas for the reasons outlined in the previous chapter. If you are going to cast your own projectiles, refer to Chapters 5 and 6 for details.

Here is the procedure that I follow when using a Pedersoli Brown Bess in .75 calibre.

Make sure your flint is fastened securely between the jaws of the hammer with a piece of scrap leather or thin lead sheet. With the muzzle facing in a safe direction, pull back the hammer to the half cock position. Give the barrel a thorough clean out with a piece of moistened flannelette to remove any oil. Make sure there is no oil in the powder pan or near the flash hole.

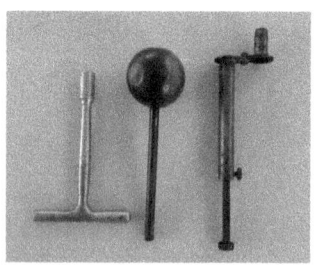

Left to right: a nipple wrench is used for removing and reinstalling nipples. A ball starter gives a gentle nudge to help the projectile start its passage down the bore when loading. A powder measure gives accurate measures of powder. Never load a muzzleloader directly from a powder container.

Pour a suitably sized charge of suitable sized powder from the powder flask to a powder measure. Some shooters prefer to have pre-weighed charges in glass vials. Never pour powder directly from a powder flask or horn into the barrel! Should there be a glowing ember in the barrel, it can light the incoming powder and the flame will ignite the half-kilogram of powder in your hand, at which time losing your eyebrows will be the least of your worries.

For larger calibre muzzleloaders, from .62 calibre or

thereabouts and onwards, 1F powder is the usual choice. Black powder graduates from the largest (named 'cannon') and continues downwards to 1F for .62 calibre and larger, 2F from .45 to .58 calibre, and 3F for .45 calibre and smaller. 4F powder tends to be used as priming powder in flintlocks. Some muzzleloaders with a calibre that is on the cusp of two powders (such as .45 that uses 3F but that can also use 2F) may find that the firearm performs better with either a larger or smaller grained powder. Some initial experimentation, recording inputs and results, will reveal the powder best suited to a particular firearm. Keep your notes in a computer or notebook.

Now, with a smoothbore of a nominal .75 calibre, the Brown Bess will usually accept a bare lead ball of .75 inches if there is no cloth patch wrapped around the ball. If you are going to use a cloth patch of, say, .015 inches thickness around the musket ball, then with a ball diameter of .75 inches *plus* a cloth patch around the musket ball, we end up with a projectile measuring .78 inches - and this will not, in normal circumstances, travel down the bore. In this instance, a smaller diameter musket ball of .71 inches should be chosen, or even a .69 ball. Many shooters are not averse to using a .69 inch ball to ensure that the musket ball easily goes down the barrel. If you want to shoot a muzzleloading flintlock Kentucky rifle, it becomes critical that a suitable diameter musket ball with a cloth patch of the correct thickness is chosen. Muzzleloading suppliers can provide patches in varying thicknesses to suit most needs. Old pillow cases can be a good source of a material known as 'ticking', for patching.

With the muzzle pointing in a safe direction, tamp down the musket ball onto the powder, remembering to remove the ramrod. The tamping does not have to be severe; just firm enough to seat the musket ball on top of the powder. The British used pre-made cartridges consisting of a musket ball wrapped in a twist of newspaper, into which was also twisted a charge of black powder. The paper was bitten off at the powder end, and most the powder was poured down the barrel. The paper formed a wad between the musket ball and the black powder. A small amount of black powder was used to prime the flash pan.

Now, with a small amount of powder in the flash pan, the hammer is pulled back to full cock and the butt of the musket brought up to the shoulder. Identify your target and then pull the trigger if safe to do so. Hopefully you will be rewarded with a visible flash from the muzzle and then be surrounded by sulphurous smelling smoke.

We now come to my aforementioned favourite muzzleloader: the percussion cap military rifle. If you have a percussion civilian rifle, then the process is exactly the same. The loading procedure is essentially the same as a flintlock with the exception of placing a percussion cap on a nipple in lieu of putting black powder in the pan. Some percussion muzzleloaders fire a patched musket ball exactly the same as flintlock, whilst others are meant to fire a Minié ball or paper patched projectile. Patched musket balls require a rifle twist around one twist in seventy two inches, while Miniés and paper patched projectiles require a twist of approximately one twist in forty eight inches in the rifling.

The Minié ball was designed by French army officer Claude-Étienne Minié in 1848. It is cast in unalloyed (pure) lead, and has a hollow base that swells up with pressure from gas generated by the burning black powder to create a tight grip with the barrel, giving better accuracy. The Minié has a pointed nose and one or more grease grooves, containing lubricant, around the projectile. The lubricant is to reduce leading created by hot gasses, and to keep the residue of burnt powder, known as fouling, soft so that it doesn't become obstructive, and is much easier to clean out.

Paper patched projectiles are cast in pure lead, are smooth sided and are several hundredths of an inch smaller in diameter than the barrel. A paper patched projectile of between .55 and .56 inches would be used in a firearm with a .577 inch diameter barrel. The projectile has lightly moistened thin paper wrapped twice around it to make a snug fit in the barrel. When the moistened paper dries, it shrinks slightly and does not slip off the projectile. The paper wrapped base of the projectile receives a fine coating of lubricant to assist its passage down the barrel.

You are unlikely to find paper patched projectiles on the shelf of your local gun shop though you may find occasional packets of Minié balls that have been cast by someone looking for a bit of pocket money. Round balls in various sizes are available from well-known manufacturers – but they are not cheap. The message is this: if you want to shoot muzzleloaders on a semi regular basis you will need to cast your own projectiles. Refer to Chapter 5 for guidance on how to cast projectiles from a mould.

There are a large number of various Minié and round ball moulds available from manufacturers such as Lyman, Saeco, Lee and others, and these can be sourced with a minimum of effort. Moulds for paper patched projectiles are made by smaller specialised manufacturers.

Paper patched projectiles can be time consuming to make. Cut out the paper patches preferably with a template, gently moisten the patches and then wrap them around the projectile. This is time consuming and requires nimble fingers so it is a reasonable question to ask why go to all this time and trouble to make paper patch projectiles when Miniés are usually just as accurate.

On a hot day, lubricated Miniés are sticky, and your hands and usually your clothing will end up covered in lubricant. This is no issue if you are in old clothing, but not so good if you are involved in re-enacting, wearing a costume that took time and money to acquire.

I have shot a Parker Hale Pattern .577 muzzleloader for over thirty years using Miniés cast from a Lyman mould. On a typical warm sunny day I could fire between five and six shots before the bore required brushing out to clean away burnt powder. When your bore is fouled it becomes noticeably more difficult to seat the projectiles down the barrel with the ramrod.

I was able to obtain a modern mould that cast a .55 Pritchett projectile. Robert Pritchett was a member of an English family of gunsmiths, and designed a paper patched projectile that was adopted by the British army. On a warm April day, I was able to load over twenty paper patched Pritchett rounds without the necessity of having to give the bore a brushing out. Several other shooters who had .577 muzzleloaders also tried the paper patched projectiles, noting their increased ability to keep loading without cleaning the bore on a regular basis, compared with loading with Miniés. I attribute this to two factors: firstly, the tighter fit of the expanded paper patched projectile pushing out the fouling; and – probably more importantly - the wiping effect of the paper patch on the bore. As an aside, and not relevant to this chapter, several fellow shooters have noticed that the bores of breech-loading Martini Henrys always look better for having had paper patched projectiles put through them.

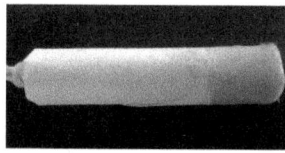

The Pritchett cartridge is a practical way of having a lubricated projectile and measured powder charge in one container.

After a day on the range, you have to clean your muzzleloader. Black powder is not corrosive but it is hygroscopic; that is, it attracts moisture from the air. As metal cools down, minute drops of condensation can form on its surface, and it is essential that condensation absorbed by black powder not be allowed to remain, to result in rust.

Firstly, cover either the nipple or the vent hole in the flash pan with some flannelette, lower the hammer, and then insert hot water mixed with either dishwashing liquid or a proprietary muzzleloader cleaner. This can be messy, so use a suitable funnel and be careful not to overfill the barrel. Be sure to have an old rag at hand to hold the barrel, as it will rapidly become hot and difficult to hold.

Using a suitable sized brush, give the barrel a good scrubbing out. An alternative way of cleaning out the barrel of percussion loaders is to fit a flexible piece of plastic tubing to the nipple, with the other end in a bucket of hot water mixed with cleaner, then using a wool mop, suck up the fluid through the plastic piping into the barrel and expel it back through the plastic piping.

Bore cleaner and lubricants for projectiles are essential for muzzleloaders. Projectiles must be either lubricated or paper patched.

Follow this up by giving the bore a good scrubbing out with a bronze brush, and a final oiling after drying.

Slightly moistened flannelette on a jag needs to be passed down the barrel several times to pick up any remaining moisture or powder residue. Do not try and save a few dollars by using the cheapest oil you can find, as it will be false economy when you discover a rusted barrel. Depending on what facilities are available on the range, at minimum I like to flush out the barrel, brush out the bore and give it light oiling. It may be overkill, but in a humid climate such as we have in Brisbane I prefer to run flannelette down the barrel, and then oil it at least twice over two days. Do not forget to remove the nipple and oil it, and its recess in the boss of the barrel, or else you may end up with a rusted nipple stuck fast to the boss. Wrapping Teflon plumbers' tape around the thread of the nipple before inserting it back in to the boss is a good practice.

Some barrels are quickly removed from the stock, while others take more time. If you intend to leave the barrel in the stock while cleaning it, make sure no water gets in between the barrel and the stock. Many competitive muzzleloading shooters prefer to not to remove the barrel, as it may affect the bedding and zeroing of the sights.

Left to right: a mainspring vice is required for disassembly of the action. A tompion keeps debris out of the bore and Teflon plumbers tape is wrapped around the nipple thread to make it gastight.

Make sure you give all exposed metal a good clean and follow up with a light oiling. It is good practice to remove the lock plate to give the internal mechanism a good clean with a toothbrush, and a very light oiling.

When burnt, black powder produces a number of by-products including potassium carbonate, potassium sulphate and potassium sulphide. Both potassium carbonate and potassium sulphide are alkaline, particularly potassium carbonate with a pH of 11.6. Potassium carbonate is readily soluble in cold water while potassium sulphate requires boiling water to be soluble - hence the need for hot water to properly clean a barrel. Both potassium carbonate and potassium sulphide are hygroscopic and need to be removed, as they attract moisture from the atmosphere. Potassium sulphate is non-hygroscopic has a high melting point and subsequently a high vapour point, and therefore leaves large quantities of residue. Make sure you have somewhere to pour out the blackened cleaning fluid, and be careful as this fluid will stain anything it comes into contact with, including cement. The secret to a happy life is a happy wife, and a stained kitchen or laundry floor is not conducive to domestic harmony.

If you were to ask: "Why go to all this extra work just to shoot black powder?" I would respond by insisting that it's fun! (...despite being covered in black muck and reeking of sulphur.)

Chapter Three

Skills and techniques of loading cartridges

A selection of reloading dies are essential if you wish to shoot centrefire firearms. Apart from dies for extra large black powder or big game calibres, most dies are manufactured with an industry standard thread pitch of 7/8x14. This means the threaded section of the die body is 7/8 of an inch in diameter with fourteen full turns of the thread to the inch. The metric system barely rates a mention in the United States where imperial inches reign supreme, and where ninety-nine point nine percent of reloading gear is made. Dies for large capacity cartridges will be found in 1 1/4 inch x 12 thread (Lee) or 1x14 thread (CH4D).

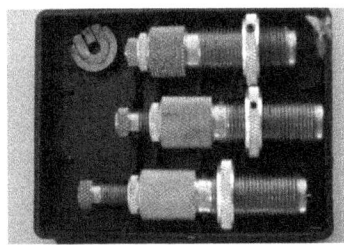

A set of CH Martini Henry dies, worth every cent you pay for them.

In most instances, the dies for basic centrefire calibres are all available off-the-shelf. If brand A is not available, brands B and C usually are. If you are wanting to reload 6.5x55 Swedish, .303 British, 30.06 or 8x57 Mauser you will have no problems sourcing dies at any major gun shop. If you wish to reload .43 Mauser, 8mm Kropatschek or something equally exotic then you are most likely going to have the dies ordered in for you. Without wishing to upset local businesses, dies that are not readily available in Australia can often be sourced online from the United States. You the consumer need to decide whether you are prepared to pay the cost of postage from overseas, or prefer to wait several months for a local supplier to source the dies. CH4D dies are unfortunately not commonly available in Australia, and more's the pity, as they make quality dies in the more obscure British and European calibres. Lee will often do a limited run of uncommon calibres for a short period of time, and it pays to keep an eye out for them, as they are reasonably priced.

At the very minimum, to reload a centrefire cartridge you will need a seating die that seats the projectile in the neck of the case and either a neck sizing or a full length resizing die. A neck sizing die sizes only the neck of the cartridge back to its original size, and does not reduce the body of the case back to its original dimensions. When using a necking die, the case will remain slightly blown out to match the dimensions of the barrel's chamber. A word of caution: if you only neck size and have several firearms in the same calibre, your brass may not chamber in all your firearms due to slight variations in chamber sizes. Full length resizing is where the cartridge case is returned to its original size and logically should chamber in any firearm of that particular calibre.

Progression from a 24 gauge shotgun cartridge to a .577 Snider cartridge.

One of the never-ending controversies within the shooting fraternity is whether to neck size or full length resize, and countless articles have been written over the years extolling the virtue of one method and deriding the other with little ground given. Generally, target shooters will state that neck sizing gives better accuracy as the cartridge better fits the chamber, whilst other shooters will say that full length resizing by keeping the case to industry standards stops stretching and stops potential case failure from thin brass.

When I was a novice I was told to full length resize every time I reloaded, and I have never had a ruptured case to contend with. The point to keep in mind is that it is your firearm, and when you reload, do what works best for you. Unlike steel which becomes soft when worked, brass becomes hard and brittle and will split with use. The antidote to split necks is annealing. By applying a controlled flame from a gas torch to the neck of the case, the metal is changed to a softer state and will no longer be brittle. Only the neck and shoulder of the case are to be annealed. Annealing the metal below the shoulder will cause the case to weaken, and it could rupture if too soft.

If you have a firearm with a tubular magazine, or a firearm in a hard kicking calibre, it may be worth considering the acquisition of a crimping die if your current seating die does not have this facility. A crimping die – as the name suggests - either crimps the case mouth into a groove on the projectile (known as a roll crimp), or it gently squeezes the case mouth against the projectile. This stops recoil from shaking the projectile loose. Some shooters like to crimp and others do not, so let circumstances dictate your choice. If you were to go hunting, you should definitely ensure that you have no loose projectiles. Relying on neck tension should work in the controlled environment of a rifle range, but driving several hours to go hunting, then finding your projectiles loose with powder everywhere, is not what makes for a good trip. Predictably some shooters will maintain that crimping improves accuracy whilst other shooters will maintain that light or no neck tension is the secret to accuracy. Never attempt to use a roll crimp on a projectile that has no crimp groove.

We now come to the next obvious stage in reloading: obtaining cartridges; and if you intend to reload 6.5x55 Swedish, .303 British, 30.06 or 8x57 Mauser, obtaining cases poses no problem other than that of cost.

Do not pass up the opportunity to acquire fired cases that often appear in gun shops and arms fairs.

Stretched cases: note the stretch marks at the base. These need to be condemned.

Naturally, condition dictates price, and often someone has changed calibres and has no further need for cases in a particular calibre. Everyone loves a bargain, but carefully examine the brass to ensure there are no splits in the neck or signs of case stretching.

As a connoisseur of vintage firearms, you will became aware that some cases, as with some reloading dies, are not readily available for some older or obscure calibres. Cases such as the 30.40 for Krag rifles can easily be formed by passing a .303 British case through a full length 30.40 Krag die, and 303/25 can be converted to 6.5 Dutch Mannlicher using the same method.

Unfortunately, other cartridge cases such as the 8mm Kropatschek require rims of the parent case (in this instance the .348 Winchester) to be modified in a lathe along with initial forming in an RCBS forming die and then final forming in an 8x50mm Lebel die. Definitely not a case to form as your first project. The .348 is the parent case for several case conversions including 8x50 Lebel, and it is worth having some handy, just in case you need to form some cartridges.

The first matter to attend to is cleaning the case. Bits of grime and grit can be stuck on the outside of the case and may scratch the inside of a reloading die, or more likely cause the case to get stuck inside the die. Stuck case removal kits are readily available but it is better not to have to resort to using one. The reloader can clean cases either by placing cases in a tumbler or an ultrasonic cleaner. I bought a Lyman tumbler in early 2005 and am still using the same cleaning media (yes, I am tight). I just put a capful of Dillon Rapid Polish case cleaner in the media, and the cases come out sparkling. There is no need to keep buying cleaning media, and a bottle of case cleaner will last for years. I use a small ultrasonic cleaner that I bought from Aldi for twenty-five dollars, and it is great for cleaning cartridges, especially those previously loaded with black powder. I still like to follow up by placing cases in a tumbler after they have been in the ultrasonic cleaner.

One good tip is not to deprime the cartridges until after they have been tumbled, as the cleaning media will get stuck in the primer pocket. This does no harm but it is time consuming picking the media out with a pointy object. You can buy hand held primer pocket cleaners for a few dollars, or you can go to the expense of buying an electric one.

Primer pocket tool.

The primer hole needs to be clean and free of obstructions, firstly to ensure reliable ignition of the powder, and secondly, to ensure ease of placing the primer in the primer pocket. A flash hole cleaning tool is essential for proper ignition of powder and correct seating of the primer. These are a two ended affair with a smaller scraper for small primers and a large scraping edge for large primer pockets. Though not essential, it is helpful to use a flash hole uniformity tool to clean out flash holes. This tool resembles a fine screwdriver, and is to be inserted into the case mouth and sent down the case until you reach the flash hole. Any small burrs or irregularities that may occur can be smoothed out with the tool.

RCBS case mouth chamfer tool; removes small burrs and irregularities.

The next task is to check the length of the cartridge case with either a gauge or a set of digital callipers. When a cartridge case starts to stretch with use, eventually it will not chamber, resulting in a wasted trip to the range. I bought digital callipers and they cost around twenty-five dollars. In the last ten years I have had only two pair; the first did not survive a free fall onto the concrete floor of my shed. Lee make a small hand held trimmer whilst Lyman, RCBS and Hornady make bench mounted units that can either be turned by hand or with an accessory driven by an electric screwdriver or drill. There is no need to trim a case until it is over the recommended length.

You need to consult a reloading manual for recommended case lengths. Cases need to be trimmed if they are slightly stretched. You will know when a case has stretched, because it will not chamber without undue force. RCBS, Lyman, Forster, Hornady and other manufacturers make trim dies and hand operated trimmers that resemble small lathes. Trim dies are super hardened dies that screw into a reloading press and allow you to trim off any excess brass that appears above the die with a fine hacksaw or just a smooth file. The hand operated trimmers are designed to be fixed to a bench top, and the case can be trimmed with a great deal of accuracy. Most bench mounted trimmers have accessories that allow the trimming to be done with the aid of an electric screw driver and this is essential if large amounts of brass need to be removed from the mouth of the case.

Lyman case trimmer, great for trimming stretched cases or minor cartridge length conversions.

Until recent times, the recommended approach when annealing was to heat the neck of the case until it turned a cherry red colour.

More knowledgeable people than myself now recommend the neck be evenly heated for between five and ten seconds and then the case gently dropped into a container of water (room temperature). This may give the neck a slightly blueish tinge. Do not forget to wear thick leather gloves, and to keep the flame in a safe direction when annealing. I used some flat timber that had doweling inserted to make a drying rack for cases that have been dipped in the water. The cases are placed upside down on the dowels and will quickly dry out in the sunshine.

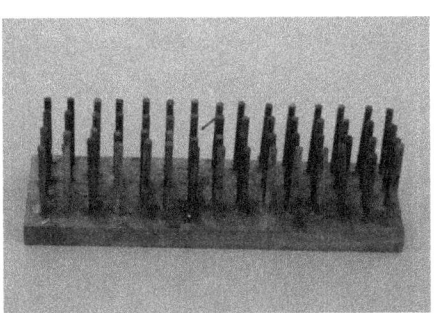

Wood drying rack, great for drying out black powder cartridges after a wash in soapy water.

An alternate method of annealing is to stand the cases up in an old baking dish filled with water up to the neck, and then heat the neck with a gas torch. As a case neck is annealed with the torch, you can tip the case over into the water. Annealing case necks should be done after every fourth firing.

To recap –
- Clean the case
- Clean the primer pocket
- Trim the case and chamfer the case mouth (if necessary)
- Anneal if and when necessary
- Either full length resize or neck size the case

Following the above procedures will go a long way to saving the cases that you worked long and hard to purchase.

We now come to the stage when a case has been cleaned, trimmed and annealed if necessary and either neck or full length resized. Now is the time to consider what powder to use in conjunction with a projectile of a specific weight.

You will need to invest in at least one reloading manual, and fortunately there are several good ones available including those published by Lyman, Sierra, ADI and Hornady. The manuals run in a logical manner, starting with the smallest of calibres and working their way up through to the big boys. One drawback with the imported reloading manuals is that not all powders used are available in Australia. This is not an issue with the ADI manual, which gives loadings for its own locally produced powders. The Lyman Cast Bullet Handbook and Black Powder Handbook are excellent sources of information for muzzleloaders and reloaders of black powder cartridges. Read the manuals carefully, especially the hints, and do not go under the minimum loads nor over the maximum loads given.

You may have an issue trying to find a load for an old or obscure cartridge. Older versions of reloading manuals often have this information but if that fails, a search of the internet may prove to be useful. Check reputable internet sites and do lots of research, as there is no way to verify what may be claimed as a safe load. Some people will put forward opinions not based on experience, whereas loads shown in reloading manuals published by reputable firms have been thoroughly researched and tested before being released. There are several very good reloading sites on the internet, so do not dismiss the internet. It also never hurts to ask an experienced reloader for help and assistance.

Once you find a load that appeals to you and suits your purposes, make sure you can obtain the powder. For those of us on a budget it is often possible to find a powder that can be used across several bullet weights and calibres. If you intend to load ex-military calibres between 6.5 and 8mm, you should be able to get away with just two or three powders depending on how flexible you wish to be. I remember an old saying: measure three times and cut once, and the message behind this saying applies to reloading too: read and re-read the information in the manual and never commit anything to memory. Always make note of the components used and the date, and ensure each ammunition container has a sticker showing these details.

Chapter Four

Loading the Cartridge

Before we start discussing the weighing and placement of powder into a case, there is an important detail concerning powder weight which needs to be understood by the novice handloader. When a reloading manual or internet site states: "Load 12.5 grains of powder X into the case", the manual is referring to weight, and not twelve-and-one-half individual pieces of powder. An individual piece of powder is known as a kernel. 'Grains' in this context are a measure of powder weight, with seven thousand grains making one pound. The urban myth of a novice handloader placing twelve kernels of powder in a case, and holding the thirteenth with a pair of tweezers as he slices it in half with a razorblade, is probably more reality than myth. Never be hesitant about seeking advice from an experienced handloader.

A critical distinction needs to be made between black powder and smokeless powder, with respect to reloading. Smokeless powder in most instances does not necessarily need to totally fill the case; some loads of smokeless may only fill half the case and others may fill the case up to the neck. There are several hundred types of smokeless powder, and they all have individual burning characteristics. These characteristics will determine how many grains of powder are suitable for a particular load. Reduced loads using smokeless powder may need a filler, and this is discussed in Chapter Seven.

Black powder is chemically very different to smokeless powder and behaves in a completely different manner. When loading a case with black powder there must be no air gap between the top of the black powder and the bottom of the projectile. The existence of an air gap here creates the possibility of a secondary detonation with disastrous results. Any potential gap must be taken up by a filler, and this will be discussed more fully in Chapter Seven.

You will need to measure out and dispense the smokeless powder in an accurate and reliable manner. There are five options available:

1. volumetric scoops such as those made by Lee,

2. beam scales that are made by many manufacturers,

3. electronic scales,

4. mechanical powder dispensers,

5. digital powder dispensers.

If you have purchased a set of Lee reloading dies, you will have seen the yellow powder scoop that is included with the dies. These scoops are available in a variety of capacities and Lee provides a list of suitable powders for the cartridge along with a suitably sized scoop. The scoops also come in a boxed set, with a chart that shows approximately how much each scoop will hold by weight for a large number of powders. It is not the most accurate method, but the scoops are always handy to have about the place.

Beam scales are the most accurate means of weighing powder, and models vary from modestly to highly priced. A set of beam scales can consistently measure out loads to a 1/10 of a grain accuracy. Beam scales are not delicate but as a highly accurate tool, they must be well looked after, and not casually handled, if they are to perform as they should. Powder is gently trickled into the pan until the desired weight is achieved. In this way, an unknown weight of powder can be measured with great accuracy.

Electronic scales are becoming very popular with shooters as prices drop. Quality varies with price and generally you get what you pay for. The budget end of the market may not be as consistently reliable as a set of upmarket beam scales, but for a moderate outlay you can acquire a set of electronic scales that will accurately measure to a tenth of a grain.

Mechanical powder dispensers were very popular until the advent of the electronic version. They contain a powder reservoir that can be altered to hold various volumes of powder, and are popular with handloaders. The powder reservoir has to be changed with each different powder or amount of powder required, and a set of scales is required to measure the powder dropped until you are confident that the dispenser is consistently dropping the same amount of powder. Never measure black powder in a dispenser not designed for it.

Digital powder dispensers are a hybrid consisting of digital scales matched to a digital dispenser, and were once a luxury. With the falling cost of all items containing silicon chips, digital dispensers are now becoming more affordable and are increasingly popular as the price drops. Once the digital machine has been calibrated, it is merely a matter of choosing the weight of the powder you wish to have dispensed and entering it on a keypad. Though the mechanical powder dispenser gives years of good service, it is likely to be displaced by the digital version in the same way slide rules were displaced by pocket calculators.

All that is left to discuss is the selection of primers and projectiles in the next chapter. I won't go into any discussion with primers other than to say that some brands are considered to be "hotter" than other brands, and you need to be guided by your reloading manual, especially when using maximum loads.

Finally, a word about smokeless powders. Some smokeless powders can be substituted for black powder in some cartridges, but never use smokeless powder in a muzzleloader. These smokeless powders for black powder loads will be listed in reliable reloading manuals and you must follow the recommended loads in the manual. Much will depend on the firearm you are using; you must take into account that the metal used in older firearms may not be as strong as modern metals. This must be factored into your reloading.

Smokeless or nitro loads for black powder cartridges were popular in the early twentieth century, when cartridge manufacturers had stopped producing black powder cartridges. But there was still a demand for ammunition that was safe in firearms designed for black powder as the propellant. These cartridges use powder that has been especially chosen not to generate high pressures, while still capable of generating enough energy to send the projectile down the barrel.

There is a danger in the novice thinking that if smokeless powder X works just fine in my 22.250, a reduced load of powder X will be ok in my Snider or replica 45.70 buffalo gun. It is great if that is the case, but some powders behave differently when not used as intended. Too light a charge of powder may be insufficient to drive the projectile down the barrel, and when this happens hot gasses build up under pressure with nowhere to go. This results in a bulged barrel, or worse - a barrel or action failure causing considerable harm to soft flesh. At the risk of boring the reader, I repeat: **always refer to reputable reloading manuals and do not invent your own loads**. Furthermore, always consult a reputable reloading manual if you want to use reduced loads of smokeless powder in a modern centrefire firearm.

One special use of smokeless powders is in 'duplex loads' in cartridges designed for black powder. Modern black powder does not burn as well as black powder manufactured in the nineteenth century, and this gives rise to increased fouling, reducing accuracy. To decrease this fouling, some manuals will refer to a duplex load: a small amount of smokeless powder (usually around 10-12% of total powder) placed over the primer with black powder on top of the smokeless powder that goes all the way to the base of the grease cookie or projectile. Some internet sites may list a percentage of somewhere between 15% and 20% smokeless powder, but in my opinion this is way too high; I advise you stick to 10%.

The smokeless powder is used to ensure complete combustion of the black powder, and a reduction in fouling. The rule of thumb is that one grain of smokeless powder is equal in energy to three grains of black powder, so if you use five grains of smokeless powder as a duplex charge, the black powder charge is reduced by fifteen grains. You need to ensure that no air pockets exist in the cartridge, and it does help if you use a spreadsheet to do some fine tuning to the percentages. Where necessary, you may have to use fillers such as Dacron, blocker tube or kapok. Duplex charges should only be used in firearms that are capable of dealing with these charges. And when in doubt, stick to black powder.

Chapter Five

Choosing a Mould

Lead, and various lead alloys such as wheel weights and printers' lead, will posses slightly different dimensions from each other when cooled down after leaving a mould. When a .308 mould is used with different alloys, the diameter of the projectile can range anywhere between, say, .3079 and .309. Some moulds are designed to give a specific size using wheel weights, whilst for instance Lyman moulds are designed for specific weights and sizes using an alloy known as Lyman No.2. Lyman No.2 is made by alloying printers' lead with 50/50 bar solder and plain lead. Moulds for muzzleloaders are designed to be used with pure lead. Some moulds are cut to use with wheel weights; you need to ascertain what metal your mould is designed for.

Taking the muzzle dimensions of a Model 1896 Swedish Mauser, using alloy.

The rule of thumb is that a cast projectile for centrefires should be the width of the barrel measured from the widest point plus an extra thousandth of an inch. For instance, if you were to measure a soft lead slug forced through a Mod 91 Mosin Nagants barrel, it may measure .310 inches. Adding one thousandth of an inch gives .311 inches. You would purchase a mould that casts either .311 or .312 and put the projectiles through a .311 sizing die. Another method for ascertaining what diameter cast projectile to use is to measure the throat, as some firearms - especially military ones - have generous throats. Swedish Model 96 Mausers in 6.5x55mm have a nominal bore of between .266 and .268 inches. Model 96's that are noted for their accuracy with jacketed projectiles have a reputation for not shooting well with cast projectiles.

When casts of chambers were taken, the chamber throats were measured and they all measured .270 inches. This difference of two thousandths of an inch reduces accuracy, and some mould manufacturers are now making moulds with a diameter of .270 inches.

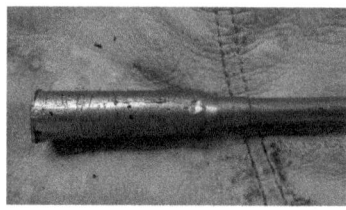

Cast of chamber and first section of the bore of a Greek Mannlicher.

Accuracy has improved when these larger projectiles are used. Under no circumstances should you substitute standard sized projectiles with over-sized jacketed projectiles... the results will be extremely unpleasant.

It has probably become apparent to readers that I am not averse to casting projectiles. Some people consider it a chore but I enjoy doing it, and do not apologise for feeling rather content after a good casting session. It you want to shoot calibres such as .577 Snider or .43 Mauser, you will discover that suitable off-the-shelf jacketed projectiles are almost non-existent, and cast lead projectiles for these calibres are not the easiest to source.

Moulds are made from four different types of material: aluminium, brass, cast iron or steel. These materials have different casting properties,

Cast of muzzle of Greek Mannlicher.

and some people prefer one metal over another. I am a sucker for brass moulds but I have some steel and cast iron moulds that are favourites. There are pros and cons for each metal.

Cast iron and steel are very similar, and in this article they are grouped together.

The pros

Aluminium	- Cheapest of the metals - Easy to machine - Corrosion resistant - Light to hold over several hours
Brass	- Easy to machine - Corrosion resistant - Retains heat
Iron/steel	- Retains heat - Durable

The cons

Aluminium	- Quickest of metals to lose heat - Not as robust as brass or iron/steel - Tendency to galling
Brass	- Heaviest metal - Most costly metal
Iron/steel	- Heavier than aluminium - Susceptible to corrosion

Here we can see that each metal has its own characteristics. I prefer brass moulds mainly because I like the locally produced

CBE moulds that are made in Australia, and I have always had good results with them, likewise I bought a custom made .55 Pritchett mould from Brooks Moulds of Montana who use cast iron and it casts superb projectiles. NOE in the United States are making a name for themselves with quality moulds in both aluminium and brass. At the other end of the spectrum I have several Lee moulds that all cast good projectiles. When the Australian dollar was strong I bought a number of second hand Lyman and Ideal steel moulds from the United States for use in ex-military rifles, and they were good value. Essentially you get what you pay for and it is best to start with something simple to see if you like it. I would not recommend investing good money in a custom mould until you have mastered the basics of casting.

If you intend to cast projectiles from a mould, you first need to determine what alloy the mould is intended to be used with. Lyman manufacture most of their moulds for centre fire smokeless powder cartridges to be used in conjunction with Lyman #2 alloy. NOE centre fire rifle moulds from the United States and the local CBE moulds are generally designed to be used with wheel weights. You can use wheel weights in a Lyman mould, or Lyman #2 alloy in an NOE or CBE mould, but you will get a small variation in weight and diameter of the projectile.

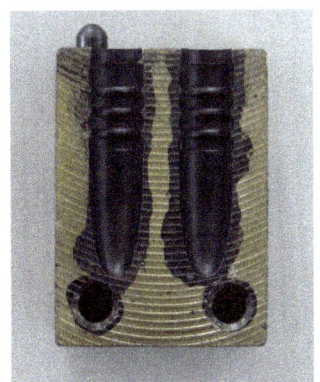

A well-made mould with the cavity prepped with graphite.

Muzzleloading moulds are made to be used with plain lead, while some black powder cartridge moulds will be designed for use with a lead/tin alloy or wheel weights. Apart from using plain lead in a muzzle loader, most moulds are fairly forgiving about what you fill them with. Buy a good reference book such as the Lyman casting handbook, do some research on reputable casting sites, and be prepared for conflicting views and opinions expressed as facts.

After all this theory, let us take a practical example. You want to cast for a Model 98 actioned Mauser in 7.65mm. We will assume the bore and chamber are in good condition and not worn out. If you are just starting off then a Lee .311 aluminium mould would be a good mould to start with, and there are several designs available from Lee. Lee moulds are a budget product but if you look after them they will give years of good service. Consulting a reloading manual, you need to select a suitable powder. If your load is going to have a velocity of 1600 feet per second or greater, you will need to select a mould that casts projectiles that can be fitted with gas checks, otherwise you will end up with severe leading in the barrel. A gas check is a cup, made from a metal such as aluminium or gilding metal, which fits on to the base of a cast projectile. It prevents gas erosion of the projectile at higher velocities and stops leading of the barrel. See Chapter Six for more on gas checks.

And now for some do's and don'ts. Do lubricate the alignment pins and under the base plate, plus the base plate screw every time you cast with the mould. These are the major points of wear and need to be kept well lubricated. There are lubricants made especially for moulds. A drop or two of lubricant on the sprue plate screw is good practice, as is coating the base of the sprue plate with either the lubricant or, in lieu of lubricant, use some graphite mixed with isopropyl alcohol.

If you have a projectile that won't release from the mould, gently tap on the mould handle with a short piece of broom stick. Do not under any circumstances hit the body of the mould as this is the quickest way to kill it. Many casters will blacken the inside of a mould with a gas lighter or a candle for the first couple of casting sessions. The blackening acts as a release agent. Some moulds need to be blackened only occasionally, and others require it every session. I have recently broken in a new mould by "heat cycling", where the mould is placed in a barbeque or gas oven and heated up to 170 degrees Celsius three or four times, then allowed to naturally cool down to air temperature. At worst this does no harm, but it does seem to assist projectiles to fall out of the cavity. The eventual aim is to have the mould cavity with a glass-like appearance.

To recap the above

1. Pick a mould

2. Purchase some lubricant for the sprue plate and alignment pins

3. Keep a gas lighter or candle on hand to blacken the cavities

4. Obtain a piece of dowel-shaped timber to gently tap the sprue plate and mould handles to release the projectile

5. Have a sufficient quantity of lead or alloy on hand

6. Have a large capacity ladle available; kitchen spoons are not suitable.

Once the projectile has been cast, it needs to be sized; and if it has grease grooves it also needs to be lubricated by using a sizing die. There are two types of commonly used sizing dies.

Lee makes a sizing die that lubricates, adds a gas check and sizes by screwing it into the top of a reloading die and pushing the projectile up through the sizer. RCBS and Lyman make sizing dies that do the same as the Lee but require their own specific combined sizing and lubricating machine. The RCBS and Lyman sizing dies are interchangeable, and will work in either brand's sizing machine. A Lee sizing die will not fit in either a RCBS or Lyman Lube Sizer.

You may occasionally require a projectile to be a size that is not catered for by Lyman or RCBS. For example, no one makes an off-the-shelf .468 sizing die suitable for a Martini Henry. Luckily, several companies including Lee will make custom sizing dies for you. Buffalo Arms make custom sizing dies for both Lyman and RCBS sizers.

Casting your own projectiles is also an economical way of plinking with exotic calibres that have expensive projectiles. One of my favourite calibres is the 416 Rigby. At the time of writing, projectiles vary in cost between $1.44 and a $1.98 each. I ordered a .417 mould from Cast Bullet Engineering that drops a 410 grain projectile using wheel weights. I have collected several CBE moulds, and they are first rate and made right here in Australia. After casting the projectile, I size it in my ancient RCBS Lube Sizer with a .417 RCBS sizing die.

To recap, reloading is an economical way of shooting centre fire cartridges. Expanding this by casting your own projectiles, and then sizing and lubricating them, allows you to use the correct fitting projectiles; this increases accuracy, and in some circumstances, saves big dollars if you have uncommon calibres. Several of us Martini Henry shooters have noticed that the lands and rifling grooves in barrels look much cleaner after cast projectiles have been fired through them, and the general consensus is that the lead seems to have a lapping effect. Several shooters who shoot paper patched lead projectiles declare that their barrels look better for having paper patched projectiles put through them.

Aluminium, brass and iron moulds.

Chapter Six

Cast Projectiles

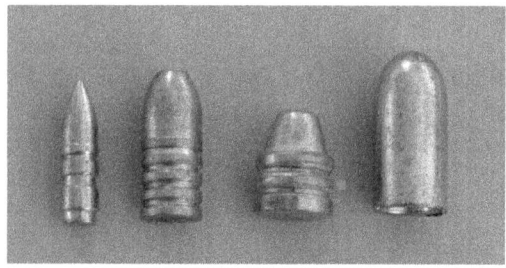

Examples of different types of cast projectiles.

Besides plain lead, there are three basic types of lead alloy available to the bullet caster:

lead and tin alloys, the tin content varying between thirty and twelve parts,

wheel weights,

and a specific alloy known as Lyman No. 2.

As discussed in Chapter Two, muzzleloaders use plain lead in the form of either a round or Minié ball. Plain lead is far too soft for use in centrefire cartridges and must be alloyed with tin for black powder cartridges and further alloyed with antimony for smokeless powder cartridges. Tin does harden lead slightly, but not as well as antimony, and tin's main purpose is to make molten lead fill out into a mould better than plain lead would. Antimony can be added to a lead/tin alloy to make it suitable for the pressures and velocities encountered with smokeless powder.

There are four good reasons for using cast projectiles. Firstly, you may have a firearm with a worn bore, which needs an oversize projectile to maintain some semblance of accuracy; secondly, cast projectiles are cheaper than commercial jacketed projectiles; thirdly, one can shoot big game rifles with reduced loads for plinking; and finally, projectiles in some sizes are not available off-the-shelf.

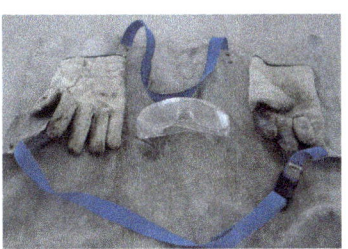

Never attempt to melt and cast molten metal without using the correct protective gear.

My reasons for using cast projectiles are a combination of all of the above. I was offered the use of a New Zealand issue .303 Martini Enfield with a tired, grotty bore that shows considerable usage to see if cast projectiles would perform better than jacketed projectiles. A standard .311 projectile did not deliver any accuracy whilst a cast bullet sized to .314 had me just hitting the side of a barn. Similarly I tested a Victoria issue Martini Enfield with a better-than-average bore and it shot very accurately with 215 grain .311 jacketed projectiles, but these are now priced at nearly 50 cents each, and it does not take long to blow away hard earned dollars. Using a cast .312 projectile that costs only a few cents gives more of the proverbial bang for the buck, **and** acceptable accuracy.

Big game rifles such as the 375 H&H, 416 Rigby etc. that are loaded with 80 to 110 grains of powder are fun to shoot, but can be punishing on the shoulder. Reduced loads give lower recoil and an opportunity for some casual plinking. (These reduced loads are definitely not the loading to be used on critters that will stomp on you or eat you for luncheon.) Reduced loads are also of benefit for teaching junior shooters the correct way to hold a centrefire rifle. The recoil of a .303 or 7.92x57 can be daunting to new shooters and reduced loads can help them gain confidence and learn how to properly hold the rifle without being distracted by the recoil of a full load.

The fourth reason, as previously discussed, is for shooters who may want to shoot a Martini Henry that requires a projectile of between .468 and .470 inches. These projectiles are not available off-the-shelf, so you have to roll your own. Similarly the .577 Snider shoots more accurately with a projectile somewhere between .585 and .590 and good results are being obtained with .60 round balls. The 577 projectile was designed to slide down the barrel of a muzzleloading rifle and this they do well, but they do not perform so well in a Snider which uses a centrefire cartridge.

There have been reports of the skirts of Minié projectiles detaching from the projectile, and becoming an obstruction in the barrel. First preference would be to use plain base projectiles, or, if using hollow base projectiles, ensure that the cavity is plugged with wood or other suitable material, such as two-part epoxy.

Reloading for most old or obscure calibres will teach you that often nothing is straightforward with reloading these cartridges, and very few components are readily available apart from those calibres used in the Wild West. The situation has improved over the last several years, especially in regard to cases and dies.

Old style wheel weights that do not contain zinc are good source for lead, tin and antimony, and can be used to cast projectiles suitable for black powder cartridges and low to medium velocity smokeless powder cartridges. Never use modern wheel weights containing zinc, as the zinc will contaminate your alloy and make it useless. Early editions of Lyman handbooks on hand loading and black powder indicate that wheel weights are too soft to be cast for modern centrefire cartridges. However, the composition of wheel weights has since changed, and they are now deemed suitable for casting into projectiles for modern centrefire cartridges.

Lyman No.2 alloy is lead, antimony and tin in specific percentages of 90% lead, 5% tin and 5% antimony, and both Lyman and various other sources give instructions on how to blend various percentages of alloys and lead such as printers' lead (linotype), bar solder, wheel weights and lead to achieve these percentages. Lyman No.2 can be used at normal centrefire velocities when suitable lubricant has been applied to the projectile. Printers lead is very hard; in fact it is so hard that it is brittle and is only suitable for low velocity magnum handgun loads, though it is a rich source of antimony, which hardens alloys.

For those on a budget, lead and alloys can be sourced from scrap metal merchants. Wheel weights can often be obtained from garages for little or no cost. For those who have some pocket money to spare, alloys in precise quantities and plain lead can be purchased from some foundries. You have to choose between purchasing convenient material off-the-shelf, and investing time casting lead and alloys. Another option that does often make economic sense is to purchase a box of cast projectiles in common sizes from commercial producers. For standard calibres, these are usually readily available, and for the occasional shooter they make a viable proposition.

All cast projectiles must be lubricated by either: an application of a suitable lubricant to the lube grooves of the projectile, or the application of a paper patch, or being coated in either molybdenum disulphide (colloquially known as moly coating) or epoxy powder coating. A projectile that has been lubricated (rather than coated with either powder coating or molybdenum disulphide) may need a gas check if the intended velocity is over 1600 feet per second. This will be discussed in more detail below.

Lubricants that contain modern petrochemicals are generally not suitable for black powder, as these lubricants react with black powder leaving a hard tar-like substance in the barrel that can be quite stubborn to remove. The majority of lubricants for projectiles intended to be used in black powder cartridges contain beeswax as the base material, plus mixtures of vegetable shortening, tallow and various other substances ranging from the mundane to the exotic. Beeswax on its own is not a particularly good lubricant, but it makes a good carrier for the other constituents of the lubricant. You can buy commercially made lubricant, or you can make your own; but if you wish to make your own black powder lubricant just be aware that some products mentioned in overseas books are not available in Australia. Paul Matthews's book *How-To's For The Black Powder Shooter* is an excellent resource for do-it-yourself black powder cartridge lubricants.

Lubricated paper patches have a dedicated following amongst shooters of black powder cartridges, but not as large as the following for projectiles with grease grooves for wax based lubricants. Some shooters of cast projectiles for modern centrefire firearms using smokeless powders also paper patch, but they are very much a minority. An undersized projectile is used, wrapped with paper of a known thickness. The slightly moist paper is wrapped twice around the projectile. If the paper is two thousands of an inch in thickness and wrapped twice around the projectile, then eight thousands of an inch needs to be taken into account. Say we have a barrel with a bore diameter of .458 inches, we would subtract eight thousands of an inch, giving a result of .45 of an inch. You would need to purchase a mould that casts a projectile of .45 inches, and wrap it twice with paper of two thousands of an inch thickness, to match the bore of the barrel. Sometimes a little bit of fine tuning is required and I would recommend that novices start with lubricated projectiles rather than paper patched projectiles.

Lubricants for smokeless loads, like those for black powder loads, can either be store bought or made at home using instructions found in books and on the internet. Cast projectiles sent from a modern centrefire firearm using full loads of powder can be driven at velocities matching those reached by jacketed projectiles, as long as the lubricant is suitable for these higher velocities, and when a gas check is used. Most lubricants suitable for higher velocities tend to be very hard and require the use of a heater in conjunction with a lube sizer. The heaters are a flat plate and fit under the base of the lubricator.

I have previously mentioned gas checks. Now is the time for an explanation of what they are and what they do. Gas checks are made out of metal; either copper, gilding material or sometimes aluminium, and fit onto the reduced base of a cast projectile. Gas checks protect the projectile from erosion by hot gasses, and the bore from excessive leading. Any projectile travelling over 1,600 fps should be fitted with a gas check. Lube sizers are designed to apply a gas check whilst lubricating the projectile.

Moly coating is generally applied as a powder to projectiles in a closed tumbler. Aerosol tins can be purchased, but these will cost more if you wish to moly coat projectiles on a regular basis. A container of moly will last a fair time for most shooters.

Epoxy powder coating projectiles is a more recent innovation than moly coating. Powder coating is diluted with acetone and applied to projectiles in a bowl, and the projectiles are then baked in a small toaster oven. I have not attempted this process and the jury seems to be out on whether homemade powder coated projectiles are capable of being produced to the same standard as commercially coated projectiles. Powder coated projectiles can come in many colours and do catch the eye with some of the bolder colours.

I hope to be able to explain the "correct" procedures in casting, as I have made all the mistakes that the casting handbooks elude to – and then a few more as well. If you are like me and scavenge lead and alloys from various sources, you will need to take certain steps to ensure consistency and reliability.

The following illustrates what needs to be considered when producing your own alloys. Several years ago I purchased 44 pounds of lead alloy that came from a deceased estate. The lead alloy had been cast in 1 pound ingots and most of the metal appeared to be fairly hard, indicating that its main constituent could either be wheel weights or printers' lead. I suspected that the ingots had been cast some thirty years beforehand.

Rule 1 – Never assume, just because you acquire a quantity of lead or lead alloy from one source, that it will be homogenous. The table on page 64 shows how the ingots, when tested for hardness with a Lee Hardness Tester, ranged from a soft alloy resembling wheel weights to a super hard alloy that was harder than printers' lead and far too brittle for practical usage.

Rule 2- The "thumb nail test" is far from accurate. Sticking your thumb nail into ingots may reveal that the ingot is harder than pure lead but it won't tell you if the lead alloy is of a consistent hardness. Refer to Rule 1.

Rule 3 - Consistency is essential for repeatability. The only way to be consistent is to be able to measure your results. A lead hardness tester is essential if, like me, you scavenge lead alloys from various sources. If all your ingots are measured for hardness, and results fall within a narrow band, you can almost guarantee that they will cast projectiles that have consistent weight and identical performance. It is also good practice to weigh your projectiles, so as to eliminate those that are too heavy or too light.

Rule 4 – A technical library is essential. Lyman print excellent handbooks on casting projectiles and using cast projectiles with either smokeless powders or black powder.

# of 1 pound ingots	Brinell Hardness	Max Pressure (PSI)	Hardness of Alloy
1	22.7	29120	
0	21.8	27914	
1	20.9	26719	
1	20.1	25710	
0	19.3	24703	Printers lead - Linotype
0	18.6	23751	
0	17.9	22852	Water quenched wheel weights
4	17.2	22002	
1	16.6	21196	
3	16.0	20433	Hardball
4	15.4	19109	
3	14.9	19021	Lyman #2
5	14.3	18367	
3	13.9	17745	
2	13.4	17152	
3	13.0	16588	
3	12.5	16050	
4	12.1	15536	
1	11.8	15046	
1	11.4	14511	
2	11.0	14128	10:1 Lead/tin
1	10.7	13699	
0	10.4	13288	
0	10.1	12895	20:1 Lead/tin
1	9.8	12517	Wheel weights
44			

The table shows how my lead ingots from the deceased estate fell into two major groupings; the first grouping was softer than Lyman #2 alloy and that the second grouping was harder than #2 alloy. The third column shows the maximum pressure suitable for that hardness. As an example, wheel weights that are not quenched should not be loaded in a cartridge that generates pressure of more than 12,517 pounds per square inch. Projectiles that are cast from wheel weights, and are immediately quenched in water, can be loaded to a maximum pressure of 22,852 pounds per square inch. The above table has been adapted from the Lee Hardness Tester kit.

From my earliest days of casting bullets, it was reinforced in all the casting manuals that the muzzle loader should always try and use the purest lead that he or she could find. Of late, some writers concede that a very small percentage of tin (3% or less) does help to fill out the larger Minié mould, but essentially plain lead was the most suitable for muzzleloading.

The caster was instructed to flux the molten lead with beeswax or borax in order to cause impurities to float to the top of the molten metal and be skimmed off. This advice is accurate and every effort should be made to skim off all the impurities such as tin, calcium, copper and whatever else is in the smelting pot.

After I started casting bullets, I progressed to casting for black powder cartridges, and later on to modern centrefire cartridges. The manuals and chat sites said to flux with beeswax or borax, and skim off all the nasties such as calcium, copper and whatever else is in the smelting pot. So, like the obedient lad that I am, I fluxed with borax the molten alloy for my black powder and centrefire cartridges, to separate the impurities out. Now, here is the conundrum that I failed to think about. On the one hand, I am fluxing to remove impurities whilst on the other hand, Lyman No. 2 alloy for centrefire projectiles requires tin and antimony, while black powder projectiles require a ratio of lead to tin ranging from 12:1 to 30:1. Fluxing removes the tin needed for both black powder and centrefire projectiles, and the antimony required for centrefire projectiles.

Let us just step aside for a moment and consult three credible websites for the caster: firstly the Los Angeles Silhouette Club: http://www.lasc.us/ secondly Cast Boolits: http://www.castboolits.gunloads.com/ and lastly the Cast Bullet Association: https://castbulletassoc.org/

These three websites are essential reading for anyone wishing to cast their own projectiles.

While perusing these sites, I stumbled upon two common threads, explaining that borax and beeswax were not the best fluxants (actually they are not fluxants!) for alloys containing lead, tin and antimony as the flux removes tin and antimony. On both threads, experienced casters recommend carbon in the form of burnt sawdust as the ideal way to remove impurities.

Perhaps you are saying to yourself: Why sawdust? What does it do or not do that makes it superior to beeswax, paraffin and borax? The answer has to do with reductants; in this instance the sawdust and oxidisers, being tin and lead oxides that float on the top of molten alloy. It is time for a bit of chemistry to explain what is going on in your melting pot. The below is true for both lead/tin alloys and Lyman No.2.

Tin is lighter than lead and will float to the top in the melting pot. It mixes with oxygen in the air and forms tin oxide. Tin oxide does not flow back into the molten lead, but sits there until it is scooped out with the other dross after the molten metal is fluxed.

The charred sawdust is carbon, and when carbon is present in sufficient quantities it forms a physical barrier between the tin floating on the top and the oxygen in the air. A reaction now occurs where the tin oxide gives up its oxygen and the carbon (acting as a reductant) bonds with the oxygen. The carbon also breaks down the surface tension of the molten metal and the tin sinks back into the mix. The carbon also absorbs impurities such as copper, calcium, iron and aluminium. It does not absorb any antimony present. The carbon is not acting as a flux, but rather as a sacrificial reductant.

The caster is best advised to use this process several times when initially making a bulk lot of alloy. Scoop off the charred sawdust and impurities and put them in a large jam tin or such like, for future disposal. I like to use a four litre olive oil tin with the top taken off. Be aware that the dross will be very hot and it will set like concrete. Take measures to protect the top of your work surfaces from scorching. When the caster is ready to re-melt the ingots for casting into projectiles, a thin layer of sawdust should be on top of the molten alloy to stop further oxidisation.

For several years I had thrown my dross and small amounts of molten lead and lead alloys into one of my mother's old enamelled baking dishes to cool down, and I had never quite got around to dumping it. When I read about using sawdust, I realised that the dross may contain tin that had been removed rather than left in the melting pot.

After I had melted down the dross in my Lee 10 pound furnace, agitating the charred sawdust continually with a ladle, ten by one pound ingots of alloy were eventually salvaged. When melting down lead or alloys, do not force unmelted metal down into the melted metal. It takes time for the impurities to float to the top and it makes more sense to let them collect on top of the metal while it is melting. The moral of the story? Never throw anything away, and recycle everything.

After using sawdust for several years as the source of carbon for the sacrificial reductant, I now just cheat and use some powdered graphite that is pure carbon. It may be my imagination, but the graphite does not - for the want of a better term - clump up and absorb molten metal. Powdered graphite is not cheap, so I will look for some charred timber and crush it down.

If the reader wishes to load some rounds with cast projectiles to breathe life back into a tired old rifle, there are a few basic issues to be dealt with. I will use my limited experience to shed some light on what, and what not, to do.

My first observation is that if you want to load a cast projectile sized to .311 inch into a properly sized .303 cartridge case with a .311 neck, you should not have any issues. Even a projectile measuring .312 should not give you any issues and it should just fit in neatly. However, I tried seating projectiles measuring .3135 to .314 and I ended up with cases that had collapsed necks and strange looking bulges. A Lee expanding die did flare the case mouth but sometimes the flare was too large and the projectiles would drop into the case while I stood there cussing and cursing.

A Lyman .303 M Series Die (expanding die) was purchased, and this gave consistent flare and neck dimension, but it still did not give enough opening to properly accommodate an oversized .314 cast projectile. The problem was solved when I ordered a custom expander from Buffalo Arms in the United States. Buffalo Arms make custom expanders that will fit in Lyman and RCBS expanding dies. I purchased a .311 to .315 expander that fits into the Lyman M Die. The expander has a gentle taper and opens up the cartridge neck. Hey presto, no more collapsed necks and strange looking bulges on the side of the case! What I have learnt is that if you want to load non-standard oversized projectiles, a neck-expanding die with a suitably sized expander is required. A custom expander costs a minimal amount and will save you a lot of grief. Buffalo Arms have a wide range of custom expanders that will keep most handloaders out of trouble.

Chapter Seven

Black Powder Cartridges

In the following two chapters, principles and theories previously expounded will be put into practice.

If you are going to load cartridges for an original black powder cartridge firearm, make sure the firearm is in good condition and can be safely fired. Sloppy actions and barrels with deep corrosion are matters for concern and should be avoided. It also pays to keep in mind that springs over one hundred years old may be fragile and snap; likewise, some components such as locking lugs and extractors may fail and prove difficult to replace. If you have had little experience with firing vintage firearms, it would be prudent to have a competent person inspect the firearm before attempting to discharge it. Also keep in mind that some firearms may have been converted to another calibre from that shown on the firearm, or may have undergone work performed by amateur blacksmiths masquerading as gunsmiths with not the slightest idea of what they should – or should not – be doing.

I will use the 45.70 as a guide, as it is probably one of the most popular black powder cartridges available and there are a large number of different firearms chambered for it. Loadings for this cartridge come in three distinct levels and they must not be confused. The mildest load is for Trapdoor Springfields which were originally derived from a muzzleloader that was converted to a centrefire cartridge. This is 1870s technology, and loadings must not exceed those shown in reloading manuals.

The next power level is for lever action firearms is the Winchester Model 1888. The action is stouter than that of the Trapdoors, and a heftier load can be used – but again, you must ensure that the cartridge is loaded to a safe level, and many of these firearms can be loaded with especially tailored smokeless powder loads.

The final loadings are intended for modern firearms such as the Ruger No1, and these loads far exceed the pressure levels of Trapdoors and lever actions designed in the latter decades of the nineteenth century. You can always load cartridges for a Trapdoor in a Winchester Model 88 or Ruger No.1, but never use cartridges intended for a Ruger in the other two. If you reload 45.70, make sure you record on the container what kind and amount of powder is used, especially if you reload for two or more firearms in this calibre. Black powder and duplex loads are appropriate for Trapdoors and lever actions, whilst the Ruger No.1 can be loaded to higher pressures to drop big critters with a minimum of fuss.

Both empty 45.70 cases and loaded ammunition are available off-the-shelf and are declared safe for all firearms. If you possess a 45.90, 45.110 or a 45.120, these cases will not be readily available; however basic .45 cases can be purchased and trimmed to the correct length. The only difference in these cartridges is the length of the cartridge. Other cases such as 40.65 can be formed out of a parent case using dies and a trimmer. 24 gauge shot gun cases can be trimmed and formed to make 577 Snider and 577/450 Martini Henry cases. Australian manufacturer Bertram Cases can supply many of the older cartridge cases and these will have the correct cartridge stamped on the base of the rim, unlike converted cases. Anything not available locally may be importable from the United States, but bear in mind that even empty brass cases are subject to import regulations and authority must be received in writing before attempting to import them.

Primers are sometimes not given much thought when it comes to black powder cartridges. As replica Sharps and Rollingblocks became available and were used competitively, it was noted, as previously discussed, that modern black powder did not burn as well as black powder from the nineteenth century. The solution that sprang to mind was to use magnum large rifle primers. This became common practice for several years and was widely promulgated amongst shooters. A strange twist occurred when someone had a eureka moment and substituted large pistol primers in lieu of magnum large rifle primers. It was noted that the black powder burnt better with the pistol primers, giving less fouling and more accuracy. Author Paul Matthews, a first rate shot and respected commentator, makes mention in his book of the rising popularity of pistol primers for black powder cartridges. The reason for the success of pistol primers appears to be that they have different burning characteristics to those of rifle primers, and they possess better ignition properties that are well suited for black powder. If you are not shooting your black powder firearm competitively and do not own a pistol, you may be quite happy to use either magnum or ordinary large rifle primers. The better burning of black powder when pistol primers are used, along with less fouling, sways me to use pistol primers.

Having said that, large pistol primers appear to be the better loading option for black powder cartridges. Mike Venturino, author of *Shooting Buffalo Rifles of the Wild West,* states that he prefers Federal 215 Large Rifle Magnum primers for competitive shooting, though at ranges of 100 yards, Federal Large Pistol Magnum primers gave the best group. What I make out from these two conflicting views is that there are so many variables interacting with each other, that primer X might work well with powder Y and projectile Z, but if you change to projectile A, results may change. Unfortunately there is no rule or algorithm that will take into account all variables. Mike Venturino has won a number of national titles in the United States, and neither he nor Matthews are armchair theorists.

Up until the 1880s, original nineteenth century black powder firearms had barrels designed to be used with lead or lead alloy projectiles rather than jacketed projectiles. The introduction of smokeless powders late in the nineteenth century necessitated barrels made from higher quality steel rather than iron or primitive steel. If in doubt as to the ability of your firearms to accept jacketed projectiles, stick to using cast projectiles and you will not do unintended harm to the bore of your barrel. Modern replicas of nineteenth century firearms are made out of quality steel but may have narrow rifling grooves suited for jacketed projectiles, or deeper rifling for cast projectiles. Original late nineteenth century service rifles such as Lee Metfords, Lee Enfield's, and the Model 93 Mausers and their successors, are manufactured to be used with jacketed projectiles. Research pays dividends and for casual plinking you cannot go past cast projectiles that are kind to the barrel and soft on the shoulder.

Straight wall cartridges (ones without a pronounced neck of smaller diameter than the rest of the case), when loaded with black powder, can be used with reduced loads as long as a suitable filler is used. Fillers include Dacron (used to fill fluffy toys and cushions), kapok and blocker rod (used to fill gaps in masonry). There must be no air gap between the top of the powder and the base of the projectile; all this space must be occupied with the filler. Another filler that can be used with straight wall cases is semolina. A rule of thumb: up to one third of the full black powder charge can be substituted with semolina. One important factor to keep in mind is that the use of semolina as filler only applies to straight wall cases such as the 45.70. Semolina in a bottle neck cartridge such as the 577/450 Martini Henry may not compress enough to go through the narrower neck, becoming a plug that will not allow the gasses to expand thus causing a dangerous pressure spike, and this may cause the receiver to fail. Dacron, kapok and blocker rod work fine when correctly used in bottle neck cartridges.

There is one possible option for the use of semolina in a bottle neck cartridge that is mentioned here only for discussion purposes, as the jury is still out: mixing semolina in equal amounts by volume with black powder, the resulting mixture again not exceeding one third of the weight of the original black powder charge. The black powder mixed with semolina causes the semolina to incinerate, without forming a plug and raising pressures to dangerous levels. Several people who have used this mixture have reported no visible rises in pressure, such as flattened primers, or a noticeable increase in felt recoil. I do not endorse using this mixture, as no proper pressure tests in a proof house have been carried out.

Now that the black powder and, if necessary, the filler has been added to the case, we come to the grease cookie and its wads. A grease cookie is small piece of lubricant that sits in the neck of the cartridge and is separated from the base of the projectile, and the filler or black powder, by cardboard wads. The purpose of the grease cookie is to line the barrel with a thin coating of lubricant, which helps create a moist residue of black powder. This makes cleaning easier, and also stops the next projectile from hitting a hardened piece of residue, causing a drop in accuracy. Wads can be either purchased pre-cut or can be home made using thin cardboard from a beer mat or a milk carton. The purpose of the wad is to firstly stop the lubricant from contaminating the powder charge, and secondly to stop the lubricant from sticking to the base of the projectile. Another option is to make wads from sheets of beeswax. The beeswax can be pressed into the top of the case neck and gently pushed down with a pencil.

Components of a .450 Martini Henry cartridge: case, kapok, wads and projectile. Only the black powder is needed.

A dissection of nineteenth century black powder cartridges of British and United States manufacture shows that grease cookies were not an original component - cardboard disks, and a filler such as kapok or carded wool were the only objects between the base of the projectile and the black powder. As previously mentioned, modern black powder burns differently to nineteenth century powder and the purpose of the grease cookie is to keep the burnt powder moist, and to stop it from hardening.

Some modern smokeless powders are *position sensitive;* the powder needs to be close to the primer and small charges will not ignite correctly in large cases. If you are going to substitute smokeless powder in a black powder cartridge, you need to be aware of the burning characteristics of the powder. Erratic ignition of powders is to be avoided at all costs as your firearm may be damaged as a result.

Assembled .450 Martini Henry cartridge.

Fillers will be required inside the cartridge if you intend to use smokeless powders that are position sensitive. Fillers that are suitable include the previously mentioned Dacron and backer rod. Failure to completely fill the void can bring about a result known as chamber ringing, and this is caused by a high pressure wave that causes to the chamber to stretch, leaving a visible stretch mark on the chamber, and ruining a firearm. To avoid damaging a black powder firearm, I prefer to use black powder, rather than a light load of smokeless powder and filler.

There is no need to use a grease cookie with smokeless powder.

Chapter Eight

Obsolete and Vintage Smokeless Cartridges

Jacketed projectiles for standard calibres are easily obtained, and can save a lot of time if you don't want to cast projectiles. Always be aware that calibres can have multiple descriptions; for example, 7.92x57 Mauser and 8x57mm Mauser are the same calibre. To confuse the matter even further, early 7.92/8mm Mausers used a .318 inch diameter projectile that was replaced early in the twentieth century with .323 inch diameter projectile. .311 diameter projectiles can be used in .303's, 7.65 Mausers and some 7.62x54r Mosin Nagants. Mosin Nagants, depending on who made the barrel, can be anywhere between .309 and .311 inches wide and when rifling grooves are taken into account can be up to .316 inches. If you wish to use reduced loads, refer to Chapter 7 for information regarding powder selection and use of fillers.

Loading for smokeless powder cartridges that are obsolete is generally less work-intensive than loading for black powder, as grease cookies and wads are not required. As previously mentioned, you must consult reliable reloading manuals, and you must be assured that the firearm is in sound condition and suitable for shooting. Weak, sloppy actions are dangerous actions, and the bore requires a thorough inspection to ensure there is no severe pitting that may cause the barrel to fail.

The metallurgy of the firearm needs to be taken into account, and allowances must be made for nineteenth century steel which is usually not of the same strength as modern steel. As discussed in Chapter Four, source a suitable powder to suit the particular type of firearm you wish to reload for. A particular powder and projectile weight combination for 7x57 may work fine in a Model 98 Mauser action but exceed acceptable pressure levels in a Model 93 Mauser, giving rise to difficult extraction, jammed bolts or worse. Also keep in mind that some powders will behave differently under different conditions, such as the presence or lack of case fillers.

Most of your basic cases for United States, British and European calibres are available off-the-shelf, but if you possess some of the more obscure calibres it does pay to purchase them when you see them available. I will admit to purchasing cases and dies for calibres that I do not possess as a form of wish fulfilment... well, they may come in handy sometime in the future. I spent an entire Saturday morning converting .348 Winchester into 8x50 Lebel, only to notice, shortly afterwards, 8 x50 cases from Prvi Partizan become available. This was a fairly simple cartridge conversion, whereas in the following appendices I give a description of converting .348 Winchester into 8mm Kropatschek. That was anything but straightforward.

Very simple case conversions can be achieved by running a combination of case trimming and enlarging case necks, with either a single die or combination of dies. Sometimes a rimmed cartridge may need to have its rim thinned, and the neatest way of doing this is in a lathe. Some people are able to do this operation in a drill press with a file, but I have minimal metal-working skills and prefer to use a small hobby lathe. It is very important that you thin from the mouth side of the cartridge, because if you come from the primer side you will thin down the primer pocket, and end up with primers standing proud from the base of the case.

If you're not inclined to venture into case forming, then as mentioned previously, the Australian company Bertram make nearly every conceivable cartridge case, and you would be hard pressed to find a calibre that is not covered by this company. Sometimes it makes financial sense, if you only want a small number of cases, to purchase them outright rather than buying extra dies and expanders and heaven knows what else... but it may not be as much fun, and you could miss the opportunity to learn a few tricks along the way.

This chapter is somewhat short, but in the appendices I have included practical examples of loading cartridges for these firearms.

Chapter Nine

Cleaning Firearms and Cases

After the fun on the range comes the fun of cleaning your firearm and gear. As I've previously stated, black powder is not corrosive, but it is hygroscopic; that is, it attracts moisture from the atmosphere. Dirty black powder firearms will be susceptible to rust if not promptly and thoroughly cleaned. By cleaning, I do *not* mean running a bit of oily flannelette down the barrel and then running the flannelette over the exposed metal surfaces, and thinking you have cleaned the rifle. Refer to Chapter Two for instructions on how to clean a muzzleloader.

Some shooters take great pride in paying top dollar for a firearm and then use the cheapest and nastiest cleaning gear they can find. Be prepared to spend good money on a quality cleaning rod and at least the same amount on jags and brushes. Buying quality cleaning gear is cheap insurance against finding rust on your firearm.

There are many quality commercially-made cleaning fluids available to the shooter, and cleaning fluids tend to be specific to either black powder or smokeless powder. If you have the inclination and time, you can make your own cleaning fluids that are at least as effective – in some cases more - than commercial cleaning fluids. An old-time favourite for cleaning black powder firearms and centrefire cartridges loaded with mercuric primers is hot water followed up by a thorough drying and oiling. Again, refer to Chapter Two for comments on the necessity for follow up cleaning. It is essential that the actions be stripped so that rust does not form in dark unseen places. Potassium sulphate is non-hygroscopic, has a high melting point and subsequently a high vapour point, and therefore leaves large quantities of residue forming a hard layer of fouling, and is the main chemical deposited around the breech. This fouling, whenever possible, should be removed after every shot, as it will reduce accuracy.

Some shooters like to season the bore of muzzle loaders and black powder cartridges. Seasoning is the application to the bore of a proprietary or homemade substance that is intended to seep into the pores of the metal. Exponents of seasoning will state that seasoning increases accuracy, makes cleaning easier and is an aid to preventing rust.

Seasoning is a topic, like full length resizing versus neck sizing, that has highly partisan views with little compromise given. Some shooters will give valid examples of seasoned barrels that perform well, whilst other shooters match these with examples of correctly seasoned barrels that have contracted terminal rust and pitting in the bore. My own take on the subject is that seasoning a barrel is fine if you live in an area of low humidity, but it is not suitable for areas of high humidity. I'm sure there are shooters living in humid areas who season a barrel and never have issues, but I would always be concerned about finding brown fuzzy fur and deep pitting in a barrel. Many shooters use alcohol based window cleaner or hand wipes to clear black powder out of the barrel between shots. Make sure you use alcohol based products and not ammonia based products, as ammonia will attack a bore very quickly and should never be left in a barrel for more than ten minutes.

There is a homemade cleaning fluid called 'Ed's Red' that I thoroughly recommend for cleaning all types of black powder and smokeless powder firearms. It is named after C.E. (Ed) Harris, who modified a cleaning fluid developed by the well-known early twentieth century shooting personality

Colonel Hatcher. The cleaning fluid is comprised of equal parts (by volume) of kerosene, mineral spirits, acetone and Dextron automatic transmission fluid.

'Ed's Red' principal components: Dextron transmission fluid, turpentine and kerosene.

A word of caution here. Acetone is cruel to timber finishes and nickel-plated metal, and only needed if you shoot shotguns that use plastic wads. The acetone dissolves plastic but unless you require the acetone to clean out plastic residues, it can be left out of the mixture quite safely. I have used Ed's Red for over ten years on all types of firearms, and I cannot recommend it highly enough. By adding a small amount of anhydrous lanolin, the mixture becomes not only a first rate cleaning fluid but is also suited for preparing firearms for long term storage.

Mineral spirits is not the same product as mineral turpentine, though they are mutually interchangeable for the purposes of making bore cleaner. Mineral spirits is chemically closer to white spirits and can be identified by its UN identifier 1268 (to be found on the label), whilst mineral turpentine is identified by UN number 1300. Odourless kerosene - used in heaters - is suitable for use in the mixture, but ordinary kerosene is also suitable. It needs to be noted that Ed's Red is not a copper solvent.

Take your time, and thoroughly clean and re-clean the metal. This must be re-emphasised, as human nature - being what it is - will settle for 'close enough is good enough'.

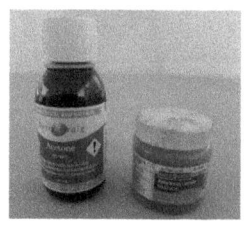

Alternative additives for Ed's Red: acetone for cleaning residue of plastic shotgun wads or lanolin that acts as a long term preservative.

Woodwork needs to be kept clean and free from residue. Do not use sewing machine oil, mineral oil or silicon products on wood, as these will slowly turn wood into pulp. Boiled linseed oil and turpentine are good for woodwork, but be aware that the 'boiled' linseed is not boiled, but contains driers, as plain linseed oil does not dry in a short time and will oxidise and darken with age. Do not do what I did as a young man and boil plain linseed oil in the misguided attempt to make 'boiled' linseed oil.

Grotty cartridge cases will eventually become stuck in the firearms chamber and can be difficult to dislodge. Cases must be cleaned, and *kept* clean. This involves removal of traces of case lubricant, powder and whatever else will adhere to the brass. Cases that were loaded with black powder will be extra grotty, and tarnish quickly. Best practice is to drop used cases straight into a container that holds water and detergent. Take it with you and this will save a lot of work later on.

Primer pocket tools are available to clean out primer pockets as residue in the primer pocket can decrease primer efficiency, and if serious enough, can cause a misfire. It is also difficult to insert primers into a dirty pocket.

Neck brushes are used to remove any stubborn lubricant or powder residue. Some shooters also like to use a neck brush to place a small amount of suitable lubricant in the neck, prior to loading the projectile. These lubricants are specifically designed powders. Other lubricants are not suitable for this purpose.

The cartridge case can be cleaned chemically, by abrasion in a tumbler, or by ultrasonic cleaners which are becoming more popular. Various pastes and fluids are available for cleaning cases by hand and are designed to attack and remove the unwanted materials without assaulting or damaging the brass. Do not be tempted to use domestic cleaning fluids on cases.

Tumbling has long been a popular method of cleaning large quantities of brass cartridges. Lyman and Dillon make tumblers that agitate the empty cases for several hours, using various media such as corn cob. Cases should not be deprimed until after tumbling, as deprimed cases will end up with media stuck in the primer pocket. Stainless steel pins in lieu of corncob are becoming more popular, but cost a lot more.

Ultrasonic cleaners have enjoyed an enthusiastic following for several years. These cleaners use a fluid medium to clean cases. I like to use an ultrasonic cleaner first, followed by tumbling, to clean cases previously loaded with black powder. As with most tasks, your available time and budget will determine your approach to cleaning cases.

If you are going to spend good money on a rifle, do not scrimp and try and maintain it on the cheap. With some quality rifles now costing $2,500 and more, $100 is not a huge price to pay for a decent rod, cleaning gear and small tool set.

Our hot, humid climate does not present ideal conditions when it comes to preserving your valued collection. Moisture from the atmosphere will condense on metal, cause rusting, and be absorbed by wooden stocks, with the result of rust being formed out of sight in barrel channels and around magazine walls. If your collection is stored in racks, dust can accumulate and moisture will be attracted by the dust.

There are four items that have no place in your gun care container. They are:

    1. 3-in-1 type sewing machine oils (and mineral oils) – they soften and pulp the wood, and send wood black,

2. general purpose greases – they trap water under their surface and consequently cause metal to rust and wood to go soft and pulpy,

3. silicon or petrochemical-based wood polish, such as 3 in 1 oils and grease – they pulp timber; and finally

4. ordinary chisel pointed screwdrivers – they damage screw slots.

Keep the grease for lubricating latches and hinges, and return the sewing machine oil and wood polish to the lady of the house from whom you originally borrowed (and neglected to return) them.

Everyone has a theory on what should be included in a cleaning kit. My kit contains the following:

- good quality bore solvent,

- 0000 size steel wool (bronze wool is better but harder to get),

- a pair of sharp scissors,

- flannelette,

- absorbent cotton/paper blend hand towels,

- synthetic or lanolin based gun oil,
- lanolin based grease,
- boiled linseed oil ('boiled' linseed oil contains driers, and is not boiled nor applied hot),
- natural or mineral turpentine,
- methylated spirits,
- hollow ground gunsmith screw drivers e.g. Chapman, Forster brands etc.,
- degreaser,
- a quantity of cleaning rods, brushes and jags.

You wouldn't take all the above to the range for an afternoon plinking session but I hope this gives you an idea of what is helpful to have for a major cleaning session, or the annual cleaning of the collection. The above could easily be expanded with a funnel for pouring boiling water down barrels after using mercuric primers. I don't like using pull-throughs, as they don't do as good a job as a brush and cleaning rod.

My latest cleaning toy is an ultrasonic cleaner that I bought from the local Aldi shop. It does a fantastic job on cleaning brass cases that have been used with black powder, shaking loose crud and gunk from bolts and cleaning brushes.

Lanolin is water repellent and lanolin-based oils and greases do a great job of keeping moisture and rust at bay. Lanolin is obtained from wool, and by using lanolin-based products you are supporting local industry and keeping jobs in Australia.

Let us say you have just bought home yet another Mauser or SMLE. A particularly filthy bore may respond well to an initial cleaning by electrolysis. This is usually a one-off process and details on the process can be found in the appendices. Naturally you have checked that no rounds are in the magazine or chamber, but you check again.

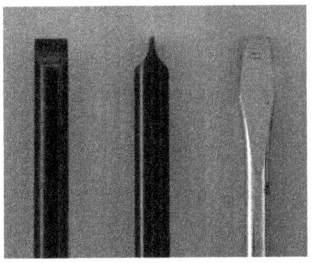

Left and middle: correct hollow ground screwdrivers for use on firearms. Right: a chisel point carpenters screw driver – not meant for firearm screws.

The following is a generic guide that naturally changes to meet individual circumstances. Once you have the rifle firmly in a cradle or gun vice:

1. Using proper hollow ground gunsmith screw drivers, completely strip the rifle. Put all screws and barrel bands etc. in a container that won't fall off the workbench.

2. Disassemble the bolt if you feel competent to do so.

3. Use degreaser to remove all grease and oil from metal parts or alternatively use an ultrasonic cleaner.

4. Remove degreaser once you're satisfied all grease and oil is removed.

5. Clean the breech and receiver and ensure all grease and oil is removed.

6. Any rust spots can be gently removed using 0000 steel wool and some turpentine. Take this step slowly and gently.

7. Coat all metal components, including screw threads, with a thin coat of oil.

8. Re-assemble the bolt.

9. Remove butt plate and screws and clean as above. When inserting screws back into the woodwork, firstly coat the screws with a small coating of lanolin grease.

10. Examine the stock, and steam out any bruises with a steam iron and a piece of old blanket.

11. Using 0000 steel wool and a 50/50 part mixture of boiled linseed oil and methylated spirits, gently clean any built-up grime from the stock. Do not use sandpaper and do not remove any stampings on the stock.

12. Keep rubbing a mixture of boiled linseed oil and natural turpentine into the stock, including the barrel channel, until

desired result is achieved. Boiled linseed oil, if used neat, tends to stay on the top of the timber and not soak in.

13. Coat stock with a wax containing turpentine and bees wax.

Hint - place a small amount of beeswax on the threads of screws that go into wood work. It will make them easier to remove if a future need arises.

Hint – if a screw has worn threads and a replacement is not readily available, wrap a small amount of plumbers white Teflon tape around a small amount of the thread. This will usually anchor the screw until a suitable replacement can be found.

And now to the barrel. You may want to clean the barrel using electrolysis initially, as per the article in this book.

1. The remains of powder are removed with a good quality solvent and a phosphor-bronze brush.

2. Carefully place some solvent on the brush and give the length of the barrel a good scrub. All cleaning of the barrel should be done from the receiver end unless the design of the receiver doesn't allow this.

3. Leave for ten minutes, then give a clean dry brush a couple of passes down the barrel. If no traces of

copper are visible, put quality oil on a fresh piece of flannelette and pass it down the bore.

4. If traces of copper are visible, use Sweets to remove it. Do not leave Sweets in the barrel for more than a few moments.

5. Carefully place some Sweets on a plastic or bronze brush (not on a copper coated brush) and give the barrel a good scrub.

6. Now keep passing a jag covered with flannelette down the barrel until no traces of copper can be seen.

7. Put good quality oil on a fresh piece of flannelette and pass it down the bore.

Give the rifle a gentle buff with a fresh clean piece of cloth. Make sure that you don't leave sticky finger prints on the metal pieces as sweat contains salt that will quickly cause rust.

Chapter Ten

Final Words

The shooter must have a realistic sense of expectation when using vintage long arms, or their replicas. A Lee Enfield that is a veteran of the Second Boer War (1899-1902) is, at the time of writing, over one hundred and twenty years old. It cannot reasonably be expected to function as well as a rifle made last week.

A good quality replica Kentucky Rifle will shoot as well as an original in its heyday, and a replica Sharps Rifle properly set up will hit a target at 900 metres if the shooter is up to the task. A shot out No1 MkIII SMLE may not have much in the way of appeal, but occasionally a good barrel becomes available and you are lured down the path of trying to work out what makes the rifle tick.

I learnt to reload because I bought a .243 made on a Mauser action, and decided that it was cheaper to reload the ammunition than pay eight dollars for factory loaded ammunition. For years I plodded along and would load the occasional batch of 7x57 Mauser. Surplus 8x57mm, .303 and 7.62x54r was plentiful and could be purchased more cheaply than individual components for reloading. Well, the inconceivable happened: surplus .303 dried up, even that of Indian and Pakistani manufacture. Enter the Historical Arms Collectors Branch of the Sporting Shooters Association of Australia (Queensland), whose members convinced me that firearms in some of the more obscure calibres could have ammunition loaded for them if I was prepared to learn and embrace a few basic skills, such as case reforming.

Despite a few mistakes, slowly but surely my efforts were responsible for First World War 8x50r Lebels being fired along with replica muzzleloading Enfields, using paper wrapped cartridges with Pritchett projectiles, and it was – and is – immensely satisfying to see some ex-military rifles fired after sixty or seventy years of inactivity.

The motivation for me to shoot something old and finicky is... I want to. I want to, and it's fun – though at times I do wonder at my willingness to spend hours tailoring hand loaded ammunition for a happy hour or two on the range.

What was the initial attraction? Barrels forged by hand in a smithy's bed of hot coals around a mandrel; the use of pins to hold a barrel in the forewood... – does an enduring affection for such archaic manufacturing methods as these brand me a romantic? - then during the industrial revolution, repetition manufacturing saw gauges used on all components to ensure they were interchangeable between individual firearms. The introduction of breech loaders challenged designers to create receivers that ranged from the functional to those that possessed more of a curiosity factor than any real sense of utility.

To me, there is a certain sense of satisfaction in shooting unusual, quirky and possibly weird firearms. Especially when they actually go bang when I pull the trigger. To come back home after a day on the range, when everything I wanted to achieve has been accomplished, is good for the spirit. What would I have done over the last twenty-five years, if these projects had not been pursued to their finalisation?

To the great unwashed who state that they do not want to own a firearm they cannot shoot, my retort is:

do a little research and get it shooting.

If shooting these types of firearms is an itch that you want to scratch – or a siren's irresistible song – I strongly urge you to seek out your local branch of the SSAA. There are branches in all states and territories, and they will be able to point you in the right direction. There are several disciplines for these firearms, and you will soon find yourself in contact with fellow enthusiasts, in a state of sulphuric bliss, after a day on the range.

Appendices

1. Loading the Martini-Henry

Let us imagine you want a Martini-Henry, you have sufficient funds, you find exactly what you are looking for on SSAA Gun Sales and after applying for a Permit to Acquire, it comes home with you. You now discover that ammunition is no longer commercially available. One option is to fire original service rounds, but I have always had an aversion to this practice; original cartridges that are somewhere between 110 and 130 years old are expensive, and firing them tends to irritate cartridge collectors.

After years of trying various techniques, I have outlined below what works for me. Make sure you have your rifle checked by a competent person to ensure it is in a safe condition to discharge. Always refer to reputable reloading books when developing loads.

Modern brass cases vary in capacity compared with original nineteenth century cases. Some Martini-Henry cases will take between 85 and 90 grains of black powder, while other cases converted from 24 gauge shotgun shells can hold up to 115 grains. 90 grains of powder gives stout recoil whilst 115 grains is masochistic on my shoulder.

The 577/450 Martini cartridge case, and the 577 Snider from which it is derived, are large volume cases and as stated above do take a lot of black powder. The flame from the primer must not only travel up the case but also has to ignite a large quantity of powder throughout the large interior of the case. Recent opinion is that large pistol primers are the optimal way to go; even better than magnum large rifle primers.

F and FF black powder are suitable and probably the most popular powders. The smaller FFF will also suffice though some shooters may notice an increase in recoil. Recently some shooters compared modern FF black powder against the original powder used in Martini-Henry cartridges, and it was noted that the original powder is closer in size to the large F size powder than FF powder.

Black powder can settle with time after being loaded in a case. I'm sure we have all opened up a new packet of corn flakes and seen how the flakes have settled, leaving a space at the top of the packet. Black powder will do the same thing in a cartridge case. A slight compression of the powder (2-5mm) using a compression plug will take care of this issue and will stop air pockets from developing. Be sure not to over-compress, as this may crush kernels, and crushed powder kernels have a different burning rate to uncrushed ones. Some people just rely on the seated projectile to provide mild compression. Be sure not to deform the projectile while seated in the cartridge's neck.

Air pockets in black powder cartridges can be dangerous as they give rise to a situation where a double detonation can occur, with nasty consequences for shooter and rifle alike. The use of a drop tube will help overcome this, as it settles the powder and allows the reloader to insert a bit more powder. I use a piece of brass tubing about 5mm in diameter and about 50 centimetres in length. First I place the drop tube in a vice on my work bench in an upright position. I leave enough room at the bottom so that a case can be easily placed under the tube and later removed. A funnel is placed on the top of the tube. The black powder is then dropped down the tube into the empty case. This causes the black powder to compact, and settles it down. This should be followed with the use of the aforementioned compression plug.

Some reloaders like to use what is known as a duplex load. This involves placing a small charge of fast burning smokeless powder on top of the primer before the black powder is placed in the cartridge. This does not significantly raise pressures when done properly but needs to be approached with caution. There are several internet sites that provide further information. The smokeless powder assists in ensuring that all the black powder is burnt off. With a service load of 85 grains of black powder, smokeless powder should not exceed eight to nine grains, and three grains of black powder should be removed for every grain of smokeless powder. Any spare space in the case must be filled with a filler such as kapok.

After placing the primer in the case and then placing the black powder in the cartridge case, using a filler if necessary, we need to insert a grease cookie. The residue of burnt black powder is filthy dirty stuff that clogs up a barrel and plays havoc with accuracy. The use of a grease cookie lines the barrel with a thin layer of beeswax or other suitable black powder lubricant, making cleaning easier. Some shooters use beeswax, others prefer a mixture of beeswax and tallow, vegetable shortening or whatever is available to them. I have even seen the use of mink oil (used to clean shoes) recommended.

Stick to natural organic substances or commercial lubricant designed for black powder, and do not use synthetic lubricants designed for smokeless powders. Some – though not all – synthetic materials react badly with black powder and form a tar-like substance that is messy and difficult to remove.

Using a hollow punch, cut out some wads of a suitable diameter from beer mats, cardboard milk cartons or sheets of beeswax. One or two wads (depending on thickness) are snugly placed over the black powder so as to ensure that the black powder is not contaminated by the grease cookie. The grease cookie is then placed on top of the wad, and another cardboard wad is placed over it. The cookie needs to be between 2 and 4 millimetres in thickness. The neck of an old condemned case is good for cutting out cookies. Cut the neck from the case at the top of the shoulder, and if you feel so inclined, an improvised handle can be attached to it. A quantity of lubricant is placed in an old cake tin to a sufficient depth, and then cut out with the old case neck. Some shooters prefer to roll lubricant between their fingers until they have achieved a pea shape, and then place this in the case neck.

Now it's time to place the projectile into the cartridge case. This is where things get somewhat involved. Lead projectiles for the Martini-Henry need to be between .465 and .470 in diameter; .458 lead projectiles are far too small and you will be flat out hitting the side of the proverbial barn. Do yourself a favour and slug the barrel with a small lead fishing sinker, determine the diameter and order a suitable mould. If you cannot find a suitable mould in the correct diameter then paper patching a cast projectile out to the correct diameter is an alternate method. Several members of my SSAA branch, Q60 Historical Arms Collectors, have noted that paper patched projectiles appear to have a beneficial effect in gently lapping the barrel and removing old fouling.

Pure lead projectiles are suitable for muzzle loaders but too soft for cartridge firearms. Projectiles must have a small amount of tin added to them; anywhere between 10% and 30% tin content seems to work well, whilst wheel weights, either on their own or stiffened with a little tin, is a useful mixture. The projectile needs to be lubricated with a lubricant suitable for use with black powder, and then loaded deeply enough to slightly compress the cookie and the black powder charge. Gently crimp the projectile into place. It is good practice to make a dummy round to ensure that the cartridge will load into the chamber. Martini-Henrys have chambers that were made long before standard SAAMI dimensions were even thought about, and what may function correctly in one rifle may not chamber in another. You are now ready to take the Martini to the range. Be sure to take a container with a mixture of water and dish washing detergent with you, in which to soak the fired cases. This makes them much easier to clean when you get home.

Let's recap the procedure -
Place primer in pocket,
load cases via drop tube,
powder is mildly compressed,
fill any air space with filler,
place over-powder wad,
insert grease cookie,
place a wad over grease cookie,
load projectile.

The Martini-Henry rifle and cartridge are not renowned for super-accuracy, but with a decent barrel they will do what they were designed to do, and with a little attention to constructing suitable cartridges they will hit gongs at 200 metres. The rifle is probably too long for most hunters, but the carbine versions are certainly more than adequate for hunting.

2. The Model 1886 Kropatschek – a brief history and reloading

Field Marshall Alfred Kropatschek (1838-1911) was born in Bielsko (Ger. Bielitz) that was then part of the

Austro-Hungarian Empire and now is part of modern Poland. He combined soldiering with designing firearms. The distinguishing features of his rifles are tubular magazines with a cartridge lifter he designed himself. Kropatschek was a contemporary and competitor of fellow Austrian soldier and firearms designer, Ferdinand Mannlicher.

The Model 1886 Kropatschek rifle is a mixture of old and new ideas of its time, in a rapidly changing environment. The Portuguese had ordered from Steyr in Austria what they thought would be a modern bolt action rifle. Bolt actions were 8mm (8x60r): then a new small calibre with an eight round tubular magazine (established technology). The 8x60r used black powder as the propellant (old technology yet to be displaced by smokeless powder). The Kropatschek outwardly resembled the German Model 71/84 Mauser that had a tubular magazine with a black powder cartridge in 11mm calibre. The 8x60r cartridge had a respectable muzzle velocity of 2,000 feet per second, and an effective range of 2,400 yards.

The Kropatschek was superior to the British Martini-Henry .45 inch black powder, the aforementioned 71/84 Mauser, and the French 11 mm Gras rifle, all of which used black powder. The Kropatschek set a new standard in service firearms, but was rapidly superseded and became semi-obsolete by the mid

1890s. In 1884, the French had experimented with smokeless nitrocellulose based propellant to replace black powder, combined with a full metal jacketed projectile. In 1888 the cartridge was introduced as the 8x50r and was coupled with the Model 1888 Lebel rifle. The Model 1888 Lebel rifle used an 11m Gras cartridge necked down to 8mm and shared many features of the 11mm French Naval Kropatschek rifle which was similar to the Portuguese Kropatschek. Overnight, all other nations' military rifles were obsolete. The Model 1886 Kropatschek was eventually loaded with smokeless powder and is said to have survived in Portuguese colonial service in Africa until 1961.

Model 1886 Kropatscheks can be sourced at auctions and arms fairs and most seem to be in fair to good condition. Unfortunately the 8x60r cartridge has not been produced for many years, however the case can be converted from .348 Winchester cases. The .348W can be converted into the 8x60r, the 8x56r, 8x50r and no doubt a host of other obsolete cartridge cases, and possibly people converting cartridges is the main source of demand for this case. Let's stick our necks out and state that hardly anyone in Australia actually owns a .348 Winchester despite the case being available.

Dint caused by using too much die lubricant.

The approach I took was to convert 348W into 8x60r. There may be easier and cheaper ways, but this method worked for me. RCBS make a forming die to convert 348W to 8x60r. These dies are not cheap but they do the initial job of starting to set the neck back and reducing neck diameter. Firstly, give the cartridge a fine coat of Imperial Sizing Wax - not too much, just a very fine coating. Imperial Sizing Wax is the best case lubricant on the market, and essential when undertaking major case conversions. Use no other type of wax when converting cases.

The next step is to place the lubricated case in the special cartridge holder supplied with the forming die. Do not use a shell holder designed for the .348W; use only the special shell holder supplied with the forming die.

All work previously done to the case will have made the brass brittle. To prevent the neck splitting, it is now advisable to anneal the neck using a gas flame and then quenching the case in water. More work is yet to be done but significant progress has been made. Refer to the photo of the reformed .348W case standing next to an 8x60r drill round, and you can see that the .348W case has now assumed the basic shape of an 8x60r.

A .348 Winchester case formed into an 8mm Kropatschek next to an original Kropatschek case.

You now need to try and find a set of 8x60r dies (CH4D make them), and insert the case into the Full Length Sizing die still using the special case holder. Now comes the tricky bit. The base of the rim needs to be chamfered. The bolt face has a rim around it, and the case rim needs to fit inside the rim, otherwise the bolt will not close. There are two ways of chamfering. The first way is to insert the case into the jaws of a drill press, and chamfer the rim of the case freehand using a file. The other way is to place the case in a lathe, and use a cutting tool to chamfer the rim. A tapered bush is placed in the chuck without the need to use a live centre. This is the approach I took, and I am very grateful to a branch member who made the bush and cutting tool for me.

Another annealing of the neck would not go astray. This is a good time to step back and think about what we have. Before any more work is attempted, now is the critical time to ensure the reformed case chambers in the Kropatschek. In my case, all went well initially, as the extractor slipped over the reformed rim and pushed the cartridge into the chamber. It was then I had a *Houston, we have a problem* moment. The empty case would chamber, but the bolt handle would only lower a few degrees.

A quick examination of the chamber revealed nothing out of the ordinary and the Vernier callipers confirmed that the case was not over-length. The only possible explanation was that the chamfered case rim did not have the correct profile to sit neatly on the bolt face. A quick touch up to the rim on the lathe and I tried again. The case still chambered but the bolt handle would not lower completely to the correct position. Branch President Michael Greenhill had loaned me an armourer's 8x60r dummy cartridge, which chambered correctly. Something was awry. I will admit that when it comes to machining, I am next to useless. I put everything away for a week while I had a think about it.

Next Saturday morning Michael came over to assist me, as two brains are said to be better than one and in this instance it proved true. Michael ran the callipers over the reformed cartridge and compared it to the armourer's cartridge. The reformed cartridge at the shoulder was 12.9mm wide whilst the armourer's cartridge was 12.3 mm and the web of the reformed case needed to be reduced by .3mm.

We were now faced with a quandary. The forming dies and the 8x60r dies could not be adjusted any further and there was no apparent way of slimming down the case and pushing back the neck. Then Michael had the bright idea of checking the dimensions of the 8x50r Lebel cartridge. A quick referral to the internet showed that the shoulder dimensions of the 8x50r and 8x60r were very similar.

Luckily, I had a set of 8x50r Lebel dies, and the expander and de-priming pin were quickly removed. Very slowly the lubricated case was inserted into the 8x50r dies and the neck was slowly pushed back. After trial and error, the case would chamber correctly but only after the 8x50r die was wound down so that only one thread could be seen.

The RCBS forming dies made no mention of the need for an intermediate die, though several sites on the internet made mention that an 8x50r die is needed. Moreover, I should have taken into consideration the small but vital difference in size between the two cases. The case was then full-length sized in the 8x60r dies. Success – the reformed cartridge chambered, and the bolt completely closed.

The Mod 1886 was designed for use with black powder with lead projectile, and the steel used to manufacture the rifle is not the equal of modern steel. I would urge caution and only load with black powder, and use a cast projectile.

My choice of projectile is the Lee .329 inch 205 grain projectile. This is a handy mould to have as it is suitable for the 8x50r Lebel, 8x56r Steyr and the 8x60r Kropatschek. If you want to use a cast projectile greater than .327 inches, the inside of the case neck needs to be reamed out to accommodate the projectile of larger dimension. I've taken the line of least resistance and settled on using projectiles sized to .327 inches.

Having lubricated and sized my projectile to .327 inches, I fully load the case with 1F powder using a large pistol primer, with a pea-sized piece of lube on top of the powder separated by a circular piece of cardboard. The projectile goes on top of the lube and again a circular piece of card separates the lube from the base of the projectile.

As with all hand loading for older firearms, the load and projectiles may need to be tweaked to obtain optimum results. If I can hit the seven ring or better, I'm happy.

Keep in mind that the 1888 Steyr is over 130 years old at the time of writing, and the object of the exercise is to have fun and revel in the satisfaction of having a venerable old firearm belching forth smoke rather than being a safe queen.

Despite the initial setbacks, it was oh-so worth the effort.

3. The Steyr Model 95

One of the more interesting surplus military rifles available is the Steyr Mod 95 in 8x56mm, rimmed. The Steyr has a straight pull bolt that is robust and functions effectively. The downside? The ammunition is fed into the magazine by the use of a Mannlicher stripper clip. This is a characteristic of all firearms with a Mannlicher magazine. If you do not have proper clips for this rifle, do not be tempted to load rounds singly into the chamber! A number of reports from the United States have highlighted an issue of extractors breaking off when rounds are loaded singly. Surplus extractors are non-existent, so be warned. I am left handed, so I find the Steyr bolt a bit awkward to use and have difficulty maintaining a constant shooting position – but this will not be an issue for right handed shooters.

The Model 1895 Steyr was originally chambered in 8x50 rimmed calibre, and used in the First World War. After the First World War the Model 95 was barrelled to suit the new 8x56mm rimmed cartridge. During the Second World War the Germans rebarrelled many Model 95's into 8x57, so it is prudent to determine the exact calibre your Model 95 is chambered for. This applies for all firearms. Some people are very lax when it comes to stamping out old calibre markings and restamping with the new calibre.

Surplus Steyr ammunition manufactured circa 1938 is available, and comes with the correct clip. The downside is that the projectile is an 8.3mm (.329 inch) 208 grain Spitzer over a heavy load of powder more suited for a machine gun. There are options available: you can pull the surplus rounds apart with either a kinetic or collet bullet puller, and replace the powder with a suitable load of modern powder; otherwise you can pull apart the surplus rounds, keep the projectiles for use in commercially available new brass, and dump the old powder on your lawn as it makes great fertiliser. If you are going to dump the ex-military brass and not reload them, don't forget to first destroy the primers by placing WD40 or penetrating oil into the cases for a few days.

Lee and other manufacturers make suitable reloading dies for the Steyr so the hand loader can load up suitable rounds. Correct diameter off-the-shelf projectiles for the Steyr are difficult to source, and a standard .323 (7.92mm) projectile is undersized for a Steyrs, which are noted with bores ranging in size from .329 to .334. Lee make a .330 205 grain mould that is stated to be suitable for the 95 Steyr, the 8mm Model 1886 Lebel and the 8mm Kropatschek. Cast loads for the Lebel and Kropatschek should be sized to .327. Lee moulds are value for money and will cast a decent projectile.

I wanted some plinking loads for the Steyr but didn't want to use my hoard of original military projectiles, as one day they may come in handy for something. The Lee mould cast a .330 projectile that I sized in my RCBS Lubesizer to .329. Lee make a .329 sizer that screws into the top of a reloading press, or if you have a RCBS or Lyman Lubesizer you will need a .329 custom sizer available from Buffalo Arms.

I loaded the cast .329 projectiles into modern Prvi Partizan cases over a mild load of Alliant Unique, and headed off to the 400-metre range at the SSAA Queensland State Complex to try out my loads. The barrel of the Steyr, though in good condition, certainly looked better for having been lapped with lead projectiles. Approximately 40 rounds were put through, and I concluded that another 100 to 150 cast rounds would make the bores look even brighter.

The Steyr shot well, and developing loads for it is certainly worth the time and effort. Aiming at the bottom of the solid 8 ring on a SSAA 200-metre centrefire target, the projectiles all shot low with most going into the space between the bottom of the 7 ring and the bottom of the sheet. Two shot low and didn't hit the target, and two shot into the bottom of the 7 ring. The next lot of cartridges will be loaded with more powder. Curiosity got the best of me and I measured the inside diameter of the fired cases – they all measured .334 inches, so a larger diameter projectile is called for. Many shooters in the United States use .338 cast projectiles sized down to .334 inches or smaller, as bores are now noted to vary in size between .329 and .334 inches.

The conclusion that can be drawn from this exercise is that some rifles will shoot cast projectiles into respectable groups, providing you expend enough time and effort fine-tuning your loads. Time needs to be expended trying different diameter projectiles of differing weights. Powder needs to be increased in $1/10^{th}$ grain increments to determine a sweet spot where powder and projectile harmonise. In this respect, it's no different from shooting with store bought jacketed projectiles and tailoring loads to match. I encourage you to have a go! You may enjoy it, and be pleasantly surprised by your results.

4. Cleaning barrels by electrolysis

Like most collectors, I have seen more than one barrel refuse to come up clean despite the use of every solvent and brush known to man. A Martini-Henry Mk1, despite having Hoppes #9, Sweets and other solvents regularly applied to the barrel, would after a couple of days look as dirty as ever. Over a long weekend with little to do I was surfing a few of the shooting forums on the internet and came across a link for cleaning the inside of a barrel by electrolysis using either household ammonia (40g/litre), white vinegar or washing soda, and two C size cells. I must admit, it was not only the novelty of this method that appealed to me, but also the low cost. I decided to substitute a 9 volt lantern battery I had on hand. Two suitable lengths of insulated wire (10 amp auto wire is great) are also required, and some large alligator clips, a stiff piece of wire to act as an electrode, some insulation tape to stop contact between the wire, and the barrel along with something to plug the breech up. To ensure a good reaction, firstly clean the barrel and remove all oil. Do not use stainless steel as it will give off harmful gasses. A thin diameter (2-3mm) piece of steel rod will give years of use for this purpose.

Step 1. Bend a wire coat hanger out into a straight length. You will need to hammer out the kinks. The electrode needs to be long enough to fit the length of the barrel and have room enough left at the top to attach an alligator clip. Wrap round some insulation tape around the base of the electrode, so that the electrode won't make contact with the barrel. I also place some tape half way up the electrode and also near the very top, to ensure it avoids contact with any part of the muzzle.

Step 2. Make a plug to stop the ammonia from flowing out of the barrel. Your method is a matter of personal choice. I use plastic lunch wrapper tightly wadded up and forced into the chamber. Be warned that ammonia does very nasty things to the finish on wooden stocks. Take your time and ensure that there will be no leaks. Better still, remove all wood work including the stock. This process can get messy, so stand the upright barrel on some newspaper or in a plastic bucket.

Step 3. After plugging the breach, fill the upright barrel with ammonia, allowing space for a bit of displacement of the fluid by the electrode.

Step 4. Connect the barrel to the negative pole of the battery. As long as good contact is made, it does not matter where the connection is on the barrel. Sights and foresight protectors are good places.

Step 5. Connect the positive wire to the electrode. After about two minutes, bubbling will occur and you should start to see "gunk" in amongst the froth. You will need to regularly top up the ammonia. I find that about 45 minutes is necessary on a fouled up barrel.

When you are happy with the result, drain the barrel and immediately dry it and apply oil all over. A typical bright wire electrode will emerge, now black with discolouration caused by lead, copper etc. that was attached to it by electrolysis. My Martini barrel now looks a lot better for the treatment. I used this process on an Israeli Mauser that had what I would call a good clean barrel. When I removed the electrode, little bits of metal that may have come from steel bullets were attached to the barrel. After cleaning the barrel it gleamed. I have also occasionally noticed an oily gel; perhaps oil that was leached out of the metal pores by the process.

The large 9 volt battery will last approximately 5 treatments, and will heat up. This process provides little electrical resistance and therefore does not lend itself to using a car battery charger, mobile phone battery charger etc. I was discussing this problem with a workmate who has a technical background. He purchased a plug-in power supply for about

$28 that converts 240 volts ac into an output of 12 volts dc at one amp. The negative wire of the power pack can be attached to a speed regulator for tools and toys etc. which costs around sixteen dollars. The speed regulator provides enough resistance to stop overheating. One drawback is that the current quickly breaks down the ammonia, but it also only takes 10 minutes as opposed to 45 minutes. I wouldn't recommend this approach unless you have to do a large number of barrels; also I have seen lantern batteries on sale for two dollars each at the local hardware shop.

A note of caution – washing soda is a very popular choice when cleaning by electrolysis but it is highly alkaline. Safety glasses and rubber gloves should be used when handling this material.

5. Quality Control When Casting

I was doing a test on a new mould with a nominal weight of 410 grains and a diameter of .468, that was intended to replicate the projectile used in Martini-Henry carbines and also to be used as a lighter projectile in Martini-Henry rifles and carbines.

I used an alloy that was basically wheel weights with a bit of extra tin added, and the metal was kept hot. During the casting I twice placed sawdust on top of the molten alloy to break the tin oxide down into tin and to re-blend the tin into the molten alloy. Rather than placing the mould on top of the furnace pot and letting it warm up as I usually do, I cast thirty projectiles that were thrown back into the furnace until acceptable projectiles started to appear.

After casting approximately one hundred projectiles, I visually inspected the them, and any that were imperfect were melted down and recast. I then decided to do a further quality assurance check by weighing half the projectiles, and grouping them by weight. The table showed that forty eight projectiles ranged in weight from 401.6 grains to 407.0 grains with an average weight 405.5 grains. I entered every projectile and its weight onto an Excel spreadsheet and entered two formulae: one to determine the average weight (405.5 grains), and one to calculate the standard deviation.

In layman's terms, a standard deviation is a statistical tool used to determine how close the total data is to the average. I am not a statistician, nor have I studied statistics, but essentially the smaller the deviation the better. The standard deviation is 1.2, so I removed all projectiles 1.2 or more grains lighter than the average, and all projectiles 1.2 or more grains heavier. The second column now showed I had a range of weights ranging from 404.4 grains to 406.7 grains, with an average weight of 405.9 grains, and a standard deviation of 0.6. The removal of seven light projectiles and two heavy ones slightly increased the average weight and reduced the standard deviation by 50% (1.2 to 6 grains). These rejected projectiles will be recast for future use. Interestingly, the lighter projectiles that were rejected all showed deformities that were not picked up in the initial visual inspection.

In theory, I now had projectiles all very close in weight, and no excuse for any flyers. I need to keep in mind the limitations of a Martini-Henry carbine with its shortened barrel.

Bibliography

Mathews, Paul A. Loading the Black Powder Rifle Cartridge. Prescott Arizona. Wolfe Publishing Co. 1993.

Wright, Graeme. Shooting the British Double Rifle 3rd Edition. S.S.A.A. Big Game Rifle Club. Produced by Ian Skennerton. Labrador, Australia. 2009.

Barnes Frank C. & Skinner S. Cartridges Of The World 11th Edition. Gun Digest Books. Iola WI. 2006.

Temple B.A. The Boxer Cartridge In The British Service. Temple B. A. Watson & Ferguson and Co. Brisbane, Australia 1977.

Venturo, Mike. Shooting Buffalo Rifles of the Old West. Livingston Montana. MLV Enterprises 2002.

Donnelly John J. & Donnelly Judy. The Handloader's Manual Of Cartridge Conversions Fourth Edition. Skyhorse Publishing. New York New York. 2011.

www.ingramcontent.com/pod-product-compliance
Lightning Source LLC
Chambersburg PA
CBHW062050290426
44109CB00027B/2787